DEAR MARGARET:
Letters from Oak Ridge to Margaret Mead

by
Thelma Present

East Tennessee Historical Society
Knoxville, Tennessee

To the loving memory of my husband, Richard D. Present. For my daughters, Irene and Constance, and my sister, Asenath Heyman.

Acknowledgments

This book could not have come about without the persistent support of three very particular people. My late husband, Richard D. Present, was the first one to suggest that I write this account. He gave me constant inspiration, and also valuable information on technical matters. My sister, Asenath Heyman, fed my spirits through my ups and downs with her immeasurable faith and encouragement. Dr. Rhoda Metraux's interest, unstinted enthusiasm, and generous advice paved my way to obtaining much needed material—especially in the Library of Congress.

I am indebted to Laffitte Howard for his help in organizing and bringing order to my text. He also submitted my manuscript to Dr. Charles F. Bryan, Jr., Executive Director of the East Tennessee Historical Society, which in turn accepted it for publication. I value the special care that Dr. Bryan, along with Dr. Mark V. Wetherington, took in presenting this book. Credit belongs to James Edward (Ed) Westcott for his excellent photographs and permission to use them and to Frank H. Hoffman, Department of Energy in Oak Ridge for providing reproductions. My grateful appreciation to the following people: Dr. Mary Catherine Bateson for allowing me to use Margaret Mead's letters, Gail Rich for her encouragement and advice, Marty Evers for many sound suggestions, the Regional Appalachian Center at the Children's Museum of Oak Ridge for permission to quote from their tapes, Dr. Charles W. Johnson for his comments and Introduction to this book, and Lee Weiskopf for her assistance. Finally, to all of the contributors—those early pioneers in Oak Ridge—I prize their friendly cooperation and willingness to share those early experiences. Extra thanks to Charmian and Waldo Cohn, who supplied me with background material, and to Ida Coveyou for her special efforts in so many ways.

Foreword

Every city, every institution has not one history, but many. Different people, different viewpoints yield different perspectives. Certainly a city such as Oak Ridge, Tennessee, verifies that historical truism. In an area of approximately 59,000 acres where about a thousand farm families had lived there was created, in just two years, Tennessee's fifth largest city. It has always been viewed by both insiders and outsiders as a special kind of place. It was developed during the dark days of World War II for a single purpose, whose complete circumstances were known to only a few. Desperately afraid that Nazi Germany would develop an atomic bomb, the Americans created the Manhattan Project to try to achieve that terrible goal before the Germans did.

The project caused a vast upheaval in many lives—in Oak Ridge, in East Tennessee, in the nation, and the world. With the explosions over Hiroshima and Nagasaki, and the end of World War II with the Japanese surrender, the city of over 75,000 in East Tennessee had completed its original goal and entered its second, but not final, phase. Thousands of those who had poured in, poured quickly right back out. They had come "for the duration" and left to carry on their lives elsewhere. The city's population precipitously dropped by half.

It was at this point that Richard and Thelma Present and their little daughter, Irene, swam against the tide, so to speak, and came to Oak Ridge. Richard Present joined the Physics Department at the University of Tennessee and continued with his Manhattan Project work at X-10 (The Lab). But this is not his story. Rather, it is an attempt by his wife to reconstruct the early years of their lives in Oak Ridge—a young couple from New York City, transplanted to what seemed to them the outback of America, hillbilly country.

They came at a fortuitous time and under somewhat special circumstances that enabled them to consider what had occurred and what was occurring in this "City Behind a Fence." While the secrecy and the urgency of the war years had not been completely lifted, many of the tensions were somewhat relaxed, and those who had been there during the war could, at last, tell others something of what had happened to them and their friends during the preceding three years. There seems to have been an outpouring of reminiscences to newcomers who wanted "to understand." Thelma Present plainly was one of those.

Her desire to understand came from more than the normal wish of a new arrival to know about the past of the world that surrounded her. Before leaving New York, she had agreed to write, more or less regularly, to her friend Margaret Mead, probably America's best known anthropologist. In these letters, she would describe social and physical conditions of life in this strange city that was closed off from the outside world by fences, gates, and government passes. What had it been like to live there? How had relationships developed? What impact did a closed community have on the residents? Even more than most newcomers, Thelma Present would observe closely her new neighbors, their lives, and their relationships. This would, of course, make her more than normally observant of her own experiences.

These letters and Mead's reponses make up the body of this book. They provide a very unusual body of material, both for this author and for future historians, sociologists, and anthropologists. They are a unique look into a city's life. Using these letters as a base, Mrs. Present adds recollections obtained primarily from people associated with the scientific community in Oak Ridge and from others who shared the early years. These are tied together by her own reminiscences. Taken together, they weave a pattern of experiences that reflects the lives, hopes, and fears of many of those who came and stayed. They present the early development of the community and the uncertainties of the immediate postwar years.

Certain generalizations made by others are confirmed, while there is also significant new ground broken. It was a city of the young; crowded, tense, exuberant, full of possibilities. It was a city of contradictions; friendly, clannish, neighborly, status conscious in some things, and in others deliberately democratic and leveling. There was a sense of the frontier, of a world to be created. There was also tension, expressed in many ways and showing through the letters and interviews, between those inside the fence and those outside, some of whom had been forced out in 1942. The scientists and their wives were not united on the questions of the use of the bomb and the direction of future nuclear research. Race relations within the city make up a significant part of this work, both during the war years and afterwards. Two particularly enlightening interviews and a very perceptive set of letters make an especially interesting section.

Now that this book has been written we are closer to an understanding of what Oak Ridge was about, what was important for some of the people who lived there. Many, whether or not they are mentioned by name in the book, will recognize the life described. Others, who are reading about Oak Ridge for the first time, will come away with a greater understanding of both of the tensions and the accomplishments of these "modern pioneers." Still others will feel that their story has yet to be told. But that is the very nature of our attempts to reconstruct our past. As we view it from various perspectives, through the eyes and memories of intelligent observers, we come to understand more fully its complexity and its endless fascination. Oak Ridge has provided, and will continue to provide, a unique way to consider our human experience.

Charles W. Johnson
Associate Professor of History
University of Tennessee

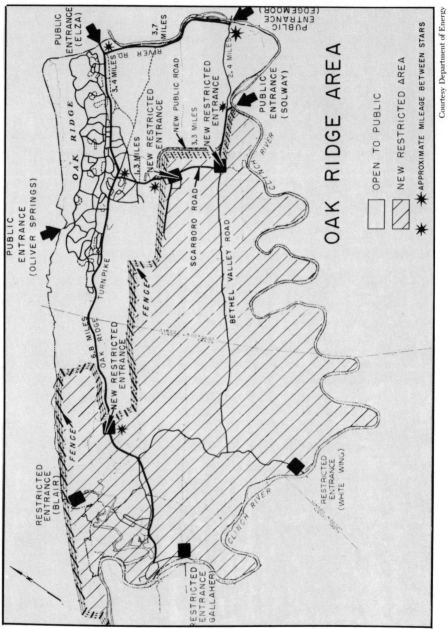

OAK RIDGE AREA

OPEN TO PUBLIC

NEW RESTRICTED AREA

APPROXIMATE MILEAGE BETWEEN STARS

PUBLIC ENTRANCE (ELZA)

PUBLIC ENTRANCE (EDGEMOOR)

PUBLIC ENTRANCE (SOLWAY)

PUBLIC ENTRANCE (OLIVER SPRINGS)

RESTRICTED ENTRANCE (BLAIR)

RESTRICTED ENTRANCE (GALLAHER)

RESTRICTED ENTRANCE (WHITE WING)

NEW RESTRICTED ENTRANCE

OAK RIDGE

FENCE

OAK RIDGE TURNPIKE

SCARBORO ROAD

BETHEL VALLEY ROAD

CLINCH RIVER

NEW PUBLIC ROAD

RIVER RD.

3.4 MILES

3.7 MILES

2.4 MILES

1.3 MILES

3.3 MILES

6.8 MILES

x

Preface

In the rush of packing and cleaning out preparatory to moving from Oak Ridge to Knoxville in August 1948, I stuffed in a shoe box all my copies of a correspondence—spanning three years—with Margaret Mead. I cannnot say why I saved them. There didn't seem to be any reason to keep them except as mementos of our life in Oak Ridge, or perhaps I thought our two daughters, at some future time, would enjoy a glimpse of what the city was like in its early years. Of course, it never occurred to me then that my letters to Mead would wind up in the Library of Congress among her archives.

To me, Oak Ridge had been a fascinating and unparalleled experiment; and, because of the city's proximity to Knoxville, I had assumed that surely the sociology department at the University of Tennessee—there was no an-thropology department as yet—had been following and recording the course of the first city of its kind anywhere in the world. And perhaps I had the vague thought that my firsthand account would be helpful in shedding light on some aspects of the spirit of the city, however personal and nonprofessional that account might be. But nothing was being done, and upon inquiry no one in the department seemed remotely interested in what had been taking place at their doorstep. So the letters remained yellowing in the shoe box and were all but forgotten.

For some years, my husband referred to the letters and urged me to "do something" with them. Finally, I agreed that the time was ripe.

When I was advised that I would need permission to use Mead's letters to me, I wrote to the American Museum of Natural History to find out who was authorized to grant such permission. Thus, I came in contact with Dr. Rhoda Metraux, a prominent and distinguished anthropologist.

In September 1979 Dr. Metraux wrote me:

> I remember very well your correspondence with Margaret Mead; she often
> spoke about Thelma Present and the problems all of you had in the closed
> community of Oak Ridge at that time. I myself was a younger colleague who
> started my professional life as an anthropologist under Margaret Mead in the
> Committee on Food Habits, the National Research Council setting in which
> she centered her work in the war years; we became friends and worked
> together from time to time throughout her life. Now I am acting as consultant
> on literary matters, together with her daughter, Dr. Mary Catherine
> Bateson. . . .*

A letter from Dr. Metraux in March of the next year said in part: "Margaret
hoped that one day this extraordinary experience [of yours] in the midst of
American life would be written up for others to know about, and I know that
she would have encouraged you to carry out your plan . . ." In 1981, she wrote:
". . . I am very enthusiastic about your manuscript, both because it makes one
live through a unique experience and because I like your presentation. . .
Your letters, of course, are priceless documents and I think you should not be
persuaded by anyone to change them in any way. . . . What will come home to
them as they read the interviews is the partial segregation as well as the
common life of everyone there . . . go ahead! It's a very good venture and full
of interest!"

And lastly: "You know, of course, that you will be making a real contribution
to our understanding of a time in our American life that people know far too
little about—as well as our understanding of one person—no, two persons—
you and Margaret."

That was March 1, 1981.

Since then the book has grown as more material has been gathered and
edited. So herewith is my account of the history, high drama, and day-to-day
drudgery of early life in this one-of-a-kind city, largely as seen through my eyes
and those of the women who laughed and loved and cried and worked that the
town might be better, that it could tame the terrible power that ended our
worst war, and could turn its use to the benefit of humanity.

Thelma Present
Knoxville, Tennessee
January, 1986

---

*The daughter of Margaret Mead and Gregory Bateson, she is married to Barkev Kassarjian and
is Dean of Faculty at Amherst College.

Introduction

OAK RIDGE ATTACKS JAPANESE

This headline appeared on page one of the *Oak Ridge Journal*, Thursday, August 9, 1945, along with a story similar to those appearing in newspapers all over the nation. Oak Ridge? Was it a remote country, an army, the name of a submarine? Or was the headline a hoax, like the Orson Welles radio broadcast* in 1938 which caused panic among listeners by convincing them that an invasion from Mars was under way? These questions could have been asked by anyone who never knew such a place existed.

Through the press and radio, Americans soon learned that Oak Ridge was a town in East Tennessee—a new town—that had been kept under wraps by the United States government for more than three years. In a blaze of publicity, this "Atomic City," population 75,000, quickly became known as the home of the atomic bomb—the city of "fabulous achievements in unlocking the stupendous energy of the atom."[1]

Further on that first page of the *Journal*, in the long center column, was a message from Colonel K. D. Nichols, Corps of Engineers, District Engineer of the Manhattan District, which read:

To Contractors, Workers, Residents of Oak Ridge:

Congratulations to all the workers at the Clinton Engineer works and to the people of Oak Ridge! You have done the impossible.

---

*Based on a version of the *War of the Worlds* by H.G. Wells.

[1]See end of Col. Nichols' message, which follows.

1

. . . .

This project has been, from the start, a cooperative enterprise, based on
mutual faith—faith of the scientist that engineers could translate his discov-
eries—yes, and his world stirring dreams—into practical process designs;
faith of the engineer that material and construction men could turn those
designs into brick and mortar and process equipment; faith of the operating
contractor that local non-technical workers would be trained to perform new
and strange tasks so exacting that they would normally be entrusted only to
skilled scientific experimenters; faith of the construction workers and operators that their supervisors knew their business; and faith of all groups—
management and employee—scientific and service—that somehow ways and
means would be found to house, feed and transport them. This faith has been
justified by the successful use of your product against the Japs.

The success of the project was made possible only because everyone did his
or her part and "stayed on the job" from the Nobel Prize winners whose
scientific theories and experiments mushroomed into huge production plants
to the sweating construction worker and the cafeteria girl with her tray of
dishes. . . .

You now surely realize the wisdom of our security program which was
effective only because of your faithful cooperation. No known case of sabotage
has been committed to slow our work and endanger your lives. . . .

A grateful nation's thanks . . . and history will record the full significance of
your fabulous achievements in unlocking the stupendous energy of the atom.
May it be used not only as an effective weapon but in the future may it play a
major part in humanity's service.

This euphoric reaction was not shared by many of the scientists who had
worked on the project—instead, they felt that the development of the weapon
had been imperative because there was information that the Germans were
doing the same. It was, to them, a grim race to succeed in developing the
bomb before the enemy did. The outcome of the war depended on it! After
the German surrender, these same scientists believed that the bomb should
not be used. Petitions were circulated and sent to President Truman in the
hope of preventing its usage. These concerned scientists became the nucleus
of the Federation of Atomic Scientists, when it was organized on September 2,
1945, a month after V-J Day.

Writers and reporters from leading newspapers, magazines, and the radio
flooded Oak Ridge, and their reports were relayed around the world.[2] Towns-
people and "outsiders" have since written books, articles, and pamphlets on
the many and unusual aspects of the city. These publications have appeared in
historical and scientific journals, in newspapers and magazines, as students'

---

[2]*Oak Ridge Journal*, August 16, 1945.

theses, and in various other forms. Oak Ridge has been "done," so to say, inside and out. What can I add about this city?

Well, what about the people Colonel Nichols congratulated, those very unique individuals who performed this prodigious task? What were they like? What kinds of lives did they lead while "the impossible" was being accomplished under the shadow of all this secrecy? One might envision them—all those scientists, Army people, workers and residents—walking around with clothespins clamping their lips. How did they cope and communicate under these unnatural conditions—husbands with wives, wives with other wives, single people, children?

And how did I come to write still another account? To trace my reason and the role I played, I must go back to a day in 1945 in New York City when I met the renowned anthropologist Margaret Mead. Our talk that day and our later conversations led to a lively correspondence between us from 1946 through 1948 while I was living in Oak Ridge. In these letters, I described the community as I saw it—at first as a newcomer and then as an increasingly involved member of this unique city.

Shortly after V-J Day, when the Federation of Atomic Scientists was formed, my husband, Richard D. Present (who had been working as a theoretical physicist on the Manhattan Project at Columbia University, New York, during the war), became a member of the Federation's executive committee and was on the speaker's bureau as well. The Federation, composed of atomic scientists from all the sites of the Manhattan Project—Columbia University, University of Chicago, Hanford, Washington, Oak Ridge, Tennessee, and Los Alamos, New Mexico—was besieged with requests from all over the country for speakers. Its mission was to inform and warn the public and Washington officialdom of the implications of the atomic bomb. The Federation stressed four points: that there was *no* defense against atomic weapons, that the United States had *no* monopoly on atomic secrets, that more powerful bombs (for example, the H-bomb) could be developed, and that this awesome weapon must be internationally controlled—it was hoped through the United Nations. The first priority of the FAS was to launch a lobby in Washington to exert pressure on Congress to defeat the May-Johnson bill, which would have placed control of the bomb under the Army, and to vote, instead, for the McMahon Act, which would put the bomb under civilian control. Due largely to their efforts, the latter Act became the law.

The Columbia University group of speakers covered the New York and Washington areas. These men and women, as well as the scientists from the other sites who were reaching the rest of the country, were untiring in their efforts to meet all these obligations. Their days and nights were occupied with speaking engagements. One of these events led to my acquaintance with Margaret Mead.

The first open address on the atomic bomb was sponsored by the International Free World Association and eighty-five American and international organizations devoted to world cooperation, and took place at the Biltmore Hotel in New York City on October 17, 1945. Robert R. Wilson was to speak on behalf of the atomic scientists but, two days before the event, was forced to cancel his appearance. My husband Richard was asked to replace him. Thus, it fell upon him to be the first atomic scientist to make public the position of the Federation in regard to the bomb. This speech, delivered to an audience of eight hundred and a roster of some of the most outstanding leaders in this country and abroad, sparked the country's realization of the urgent necessity to "listen" to the scientists.

The late Gregory Bateson approached Richard after one of these lavish affairs. Gregory, also a distinguished anthropologist and Margaret Mead's husband at that time, had been invited to write a two-part article for the *Bulletin of Atomic Scientists*,[3] and wished to discuss scientific details with someone who had been involved with the Manhattan Project. The two men had many informational meetings, participated jointly in radio programs, and became good friends. Margaret Mead, too, was interested and joined them on a few occasions. (In her autobiography, *Blackberry Winter*,[4] she wrote, "The atomic bomb exploded over Hiroshima in the summer of 1945. At that point I tore up every page of a book I had nearly finished. Every sentence was out of date. We had entered a new age.")

In January 1946, Richard accepted an invitation to join the physics department at the University of Tennessee in Knoxville and also to continue with the Manhattan Project as a part-time consultant to the X-10 Laboratory in Oak Ridge. We decided to live in Oak Ridge instead of in Knoxville. For my part, I viewed the move with much trepidation. My whole world had been centered in New York City—my family, friends, work, the cultural life, and all the excitement and glamour of hobnobbing with distinguished people and celebrities at dinners and banquets at elegant hotels through the activities of the Federation of Atomic Scientists.[5] And here I was, moving to a mysterious little town stuck in the hills of East Tennessee!

It was even more dismaying when a prankish friend, who had visited Oak Ridge, tried to fool us into believing dire things about the city. We would probably be assigned a tiny, boxlike house—perhaps on stilts—with a pot-bellied stove plumb in the middle of the living room. We might be lucky enough to have an indoor toilet and running water. Our clothing would be continuously splattered with red mud, and no amount of washings would quite

---

[3]*Bulletin of the Atomic Scientists*, September 1, 1946, Part 1, p. 10; Part 2, following issue.

[4]Margaret Mead, *Blackberry Winter* (New York, 1972), 296.

[5]Subsequently the FAS was enlarged to include scientists who had not worked on the Manhattan Project, and the name was changed to the Federation of American Scientists.

rid them of stains which would mark us as Oak Ridgers. Many rough people lived in the town, and we would have to keep our mouths shut and be wary of strangers at all times. We would be virtual prisoners within the gates—with little freedom to come and go and with soldiers watching our every move. Why, I might even have to bake our own bread! To a big-city apartment-dweller, this frightened me as much as anything else.

I tried to put up a brave front, but my mother was visibly shaken. Shortly before we moved, she visited a neighbor and, wringing her hands, poured out her fears about the hardships facing us. "They are going to this strange place in the middle of nowhere. Who knows what might happen to them!" she wept. Her friend laughed and said, "Stop worrying—someone has been pulling her leg. *My* daughter has been living in Oak Ridge since 1943. I have visited her a few times, and it's a lovely town. People are very friendly."

When Margaret Mead heard we were moving to Oak Ridge, she suggested that a luncheon meeting with me be arranged at the American Museum of Natural History. Since she was professionally interested in "new communities" and "closed communities"[6] and because Oak Ridge was such a phenomenon, she wanted to learn more about this new, unprecedented, gated city. Even "Monumental Margaret"[7] could not gain admittance there without an invitation!

I was somewhat apprehensive at the prospect of meeting Margaret. My fears were needless, for she was a pleasant, unpretentious and warm woman who, very shortly, put me completely at ease. Wasting little time on the amenities, she launched me into an exciting venture—the effect of which still remains. Was I interested in writing her frequent, informal letters about my impressions of the daily life in Oak Ridge and the effects of the unusual environment on the people of this uncommon community? Her proposal both flabbergasted and thrilled me. I expressed some doubts, owing to my lack of formal training for such a task, but agreed to give it a try. Oak Ridge now began to loom in my mind as an anthropologist's dream, and the prospect of living there immediately looked brighter and, certainly, more challenging.

Before we moved to Oak Ridge, Richard briefed me on the role of this atomic city:

> Oak Ridge was only one part of the complex that constituted the Manhattan Project which "was designated the Manhattan District and was officially established on August 13, 1942"[8] for the purpose of creating an atomic bomb.

---

[6]According to Dr. Rhoda Metraux, an esteemed anthropologist and Margaret's long-time friend and collaborator.

[7]As she was described in the *Oak Ridge Journal* editorial following her initial visit to Oak Ridge in May 1964.

[8]Quote from Henry D. Smyth, *Official Report, Atomic Energy for Military Purposes* (Princeton, New Jersey, 1945), 83.

There were, actually, three Atomic cities—Los Alamos, Hanford, and Oak Ridge.[9] The three main laboratories in Oak Ridge were:

X-10 A research facility in which theoretical and experimental work on nuclear reactors and properties of plutonium were investigated. The experimentation was done on a pilot nuclear reactor which operated at a very low power level.

K-25 a huge plant for the production of Uranium-235 by the method of gaseous diffusion.

Y-12 A large plant for production of U^{235} by electromagnetic methods.

The Oak Ridge site was selected because of its proximity to the Tennessee Valley Authority with its cheap power, seclusion and size of the area, and its sparse population.

As for the other sites: research was done mainly at Columbia University and at X-10 in Oak Ridge. The reactor research was conducted at the University of Chicago. Bomb research and development were done at Los Alamos. Hanford, Washington, was purely a production site for plutonium.

The first official account documenting the history of the Manhattan Project[10] was the Smyth Report. Because of its importance and accuracy, this report has been widely read and used for reference purposes. In it, Smyth details how Roosevelt was persuaded to sanction the Project through the combined efforts of some of the most prominent American and European physicists. Crucial experiments which established the feasibility of a fission reaction leading to an atomic bomb were carried out in the work of Enrico Fermi and Leo Szilard. Szilard persuaded Eugene Wigner to approach Albert Einstein, and to prevail upon him to write a letter[11] to Roosevelt. Alexander Sachs presented this letter to Roosevelt and convinced him of the urgency for setting up a meeting and, eventually, a committee for discussion and suitable action.

As it happened, we arrived in Oak Ridge at a propitious time. It was a turning point. With the war so recently ended, the energy and effort of the war years were still uppermost in the minds of those who had lived there during that time. These people had been pent up until V-J Day. Now, except for top secrets, came a tremendous release from all the hush-hush. The pioneers of the atomic bomb could finally talk more openly and with relish about their city. They welcomed every opportunity to recount anecdotes of their trials and tribulations. Newcomers were equally avid to learn about their adopted city.

---

[9]Also called the Clinton Engineer Works.

[10]Many people have wondered (and perhaps assumed) whether the Manhattan Project was so named because it might have emanated from the New York metropolis. It was just a name chosen as an umbrella for the whole project.

[11]The original letter from Einstein to Roosevelt is in the Roosevelt Museum in Hyde Park, New York. A facsimile may be seen in the American Museum of Science and Energy in Oak Ridge.

In less than a week I gleaned many basic details. For example, we found out that some of the things our friend had warned us about were true. There *were* areas with small, square houses on stilts. There *were* living quarters without indoor plumbing. There *were* gates, badges, and passes needed to get in and out of town, guards vigilantly patrolling the seven gates, Army control with its accompanying regimentation and paternalism, segregation—even slums. There also was the fear of expressing open criticism against certain practices. Nevertheless, we found that the advantages were numerous and that the good things tended to outweigh the bad.

The vigor and enthusiasm of this still raw, newly carved out city of 75,000 people struck me right away. The youthfulness of the population astounded me. Almost everyone had left behind all family ties—their parents, grandparents, relatives, and friends. All had come on a temporary basis and expected to depart when their mission was accomplished.

Within this fenced city there was during and after the war still another secret area, restricted entirely to the scientific personnel, and its purpose known only to a handful of people. Rumors had abounded. Despite these speculations (and some unfavorable reactions and complaints by the natives), the conspiracy of silence had lasted throughout the war.

On first sight, one could not help being impressed by the natural beauty and setting of Oak Ridge. Nearby were the ranges of the Cumberland Mountains and, in the distance, the horizons of the Great Smoky Mountains. In this long, narrow and hilly government reservation with its layers of winding ridges, the neat and tidy residential section had thousands of look-alike, white, boxlike houses with small porches; half were mirror images of each other and were differentiated only in size. There was no semblance of grandeur or wealth. These houses were reserved for the married scientists and the few top people. The size of the family determined the number of bedrooms a resident could have. The rest of the city (planned by the firm of Skidmore, Owings and Merrill, a Boston architectural firm) was laid out in numerous subdivisions, each with its own species of dwelling. In descending rank there were efficiency apartments, dormitories, flattops, victory cottages, trailers, and barracks. At the lowest end of the scale was the bleak, racially segregated hutment section—the built-in slums.

Oak Ridge was clearly a divided and class-conscious city from its very inception—but not in the usual sense. The upper echelon was composed of a large number of highly educated scientists, engineers, and a small number of leading Army people and administrators; they had been drawn from all parts of the country and usually from cosmopolitan cities. On the other hand, thousands of people had been brought in from the Southern Appalachian and rural towns to provide essential services to the community. Many were unskilled and had had little education. Oak Ridge was different from most other cities in not having many of the usual classes of society: elite, old families or landed gentry, prominent businessmen, strong professional guilds of doctors or law-yers—all were absent. For once the scientists, most of them former professors and commonly called eggheads, were the privileged and highest paid mem-bers of the community! This unexampled city differed, too, in that the Army was in complete command. The Army had overall charge of providing hous-ing, medical care, recreation, sports, and other needs. Most services, such as banks and businesses, were operated on a concession basis and only with Army approval. Housing was rented on a flat-fee basis that included all utilities and was allotted according to job classifications and salaries.

In spite of the regimentation, the citizens promoted much activity of an intellectual and cultural nature, particularly in the arts. Still, something disturbed me about the apparent acceptance of and resignation to the Army's authority. The guards at the gates and the required display of passes to move in or out of the city were taken as facts of life. Even more pervasive was the feeling that the gates protected the insiders from a possible invasion by the outside world. However, the aura of secrecy that had permeated the communi-ty had created a common bond, resulting in a tightly knit city where everyone was wholeheartedly involved in whatever it was that might shorten the war.

These were my first impressions, and, as we settled into Oak Ridge, more and more fascinating aspects emerged about this singular, many-faceted city. To reinforce my account of Oak Ridge, I have augmented the "Dear Margaret" letters with random reminiscences, gleaned from interviews with a number of early settlers who still reside there. Particularly important are the memories of a representative group of women. I have also turned the clock back to add a few recollections of my own in what is, basically, an extremely personal account. While the scientists explored the realms of the Manhattan Project, the women of Oak Ridge coped with the primitive conditions of an entirely new environment and an alien way of life. They were exceedingly supportive under trying circumstances, considering that they bore almost the sole re-sponsibility for "making do." And, in most cases, they did so with good cheer!

Part I
Beginnings

Letter I

Now what? An adventure! A prolonged vacation! Or a painful transformation from a city to a country person? These thoughts ran through my mind when I, with my husband Richard, moved to Oak Ridge in 1946.

We were given a plain, but not unattractive, room in the Guest House (now the Alexander Hotel), where we lived until our housing assignment came through. I immediately had the sense of being at a Southern resort or a summer camp. The tennis courts in front were filled with players. Automobiles bore license plates from all parts from the country. Comfortable rockers on the long porch, running the width of the white wooden building, were an invitation to relax.

Before long, I was one of the many women who sat on the porch and rocked—feeling utterly unrelaxed. Small children were swarming all around, darting in and out of the lobby, and we didn't really have the leisure to socialize. Our basic preoccupation was to calm our displaced offspring, who were at loose ends and, in general, getting into each other's hair. Further inhibiting us was the fact that not only were we women strangers to one another but we all knew better than to ask personal questions—or even to gossip.

While the Guest House was a stopover for most newcomers, it also served overnight guests. I learned later that world-famous scientists and executives had "slept" there—such personages as Dr. J. Robert Oppenheimer, Dr. Harold Urey, Dr. Eugene Wigner, Dr. Arthur H. Compton, and other notables. According to George O. (Gus) Robinson, Jr., in his "The Oak Ridge Story," they were "all moving like shadows through the mysterious recesses of the plants, unrecognized by thousands who were building what they, the

11

scientists, had planned. For security reasons, the scientists went under assumed names—Dr. Fermi, for example, was 'Farmer,' Dr. Compton 'Cosmos' and (Ernest) Lawrence 'Lawson'."

The daughter of my mother's friend welcomed me to Oak Ridge, and other wives of Richard's colleagues came around to greet me. I was impatient to get settled into whatever our new abode would turn out to be.

How vividly I recall our first day and night in our first house! Dick had been born and reared in New York City and had been an apartment-dweller all his life. I, too, had grown up in apartments since I was ten years old. How would we adjust to this alien type of shelter?

The moment we received word that our furniture had arrived, we abandoned the Guest House with no regrets. But, in a way, perhaps our stay there had served a useful purpose. We were so fed up with the anonymity of hotel life that almost anything was bound to be better. Lacking a car and due to the kindness of friends (mentioned in the letter which follows) who had been established in Oak Ridge since its beginning and who already knew the ropes, we were chauffeured to our empty cemesto[1] B house.

Though it was nicely situated on top of one of the ridges, the house was bare. But not the refrigerator—it had been filled with home-baked goodies, casseroles and enough staples to last until we could get our bearings.

We sat on our luggage on the porch, while waiting for the van, and gazed in wonder at the spectacular view of the distant Great Smoky Mountains. The house was surprisingly attractive and appeared more than suitable for our needs, the more so since we were still nervous about the warning that we might be assigned to a flattop with a pot-bellied stove smack in the living room. I was especially intrigued with the fireplace, surrounded by red brick, in the spacious living room. I had time to ponder where everything should be placed and to think about all the things that needed to be done to make the house livable. No doors to the closets—they would have to have some kind of hanging—umpteen windows to be curtained. Well, I had learned to sew for "Bundles for Britain" during the war. I would manage something simple. Maybe I could borrow or rent a sewing machine. Was material available in the city? The previous tenant had wisely chosen an all-white interior. Good! No battle of colors with our hodgepodge possessions. By the time the movers arrived and installed our furnishings, it was late afternoon.

A quick examination and a few thumps on the keys satisfied me that the

---

[1]Cemesto houses had outer walls of a material made by bonding two one-eighth-inch-thick pieces of asbestos board to an inch-and-a-quarter-thick core of Cellotex rigid insulating board. They were some of the earliest precut houses in the country and were expected to last twenty-five years. But they still stand, and as Dorothy Denn wrote in the town's newspaper, *The Oak Ridger*, in March of 1982, "those 3050 once look-alike houses have taken on individual personalities" with bay windows, brick exteriors, and California bungalow or colonial facades.

piano had survived the long trip. We had a hasty supper spread out on the top of a crate, sitting on cartons. Then we busied ourselves getting beds and sleeping paraphernalia ready. I had already practiced boiling some water to get accustomed to the electric stove, which was to alter my cooking habits.

After dusk the house became damp and chilly. Dick said that he would start a fire in the furnace. There was plenty of coal and enough cartons to start it up. It started up, all right, and almost instantly the house began to fill up with smoke. We doused the coals with water.

"Well, no point in fooling around with the furnace until I get some instruction. Anyway, we can get a fire going in the fireplace. It will be cozier," he said.

That idea sputtered out in a hurry when smoke started billowing out again— this time from the fireplace. Sweaters and coats filled the bill until bedtime.

While he was fooling around with the heating problems, I hauled out the typewriter and dashed off Letter No. I to Margaret Mead while my first week's impressions were still fresh.

Irene, our 1½-year-old, was getting fretful, and when we put her in her crib, she was afraid to sleep in the dark. There was a wall fixture over the bed with a bright, bare bulb. I turned the light on, but put a pair of her panties over it to dim the room. We turned in shortly after, mainly to get under warm covers. Sometime in the middle of the night, I was awakened by a peculiarly unpleasant smell. I started searching the house and my nose led me to Irene's room. On top of the bulb was a pair of black, smoking panties! So began our adjustment. Who would have dreamed that a 60-watt bulb could be so destructive?

Here is that letter to Margaret Mead, written eight days after we arrived in Oak Ridge:

March 13, 1946

Dear Margaret,
    Whew!
    Try to imagine a huge summer camp resort, an Army camp, a city of industrial workers and a college campus all rolled up into one. That is my first impression of Oak Ridge. A fantastic, unreal and dizzy sort of place.
    We arrived a week ago by plane, and I remember my first apprehension— almost panic—about meeting the military regulations. I think I was slightly disappointed. It felt like nothing more than paying a fare at a toll bridge. A cursory glance at our passes, no questions asked, no baggage examined, etc. The first annoyance in that respect came a few days later when "leaving the area" for a visit to Knoxville. The bus stopped just inside the gate and a Military Policeman hopped on and examined all of the passengers' badges and passes. Ugh! A very unpleasant reaction. Incidentally, all Negroes sit in the back of the buses and have a separate waiting room.
    Our furniture was delayed several days, and we stayed at the Guest House, which is the only hotel here and is a clearance place for others in our position,

people waiting to be assigned homes, wives waiting for their husbands to get their discharge from the Army, and just plain guests. One is overwhelmed with southern hospitality. It seems as if most of the people who work in restaurants, stores and shops here are decidedly southern. I understand they were imported from nearby cities. And at first the feeling is that this town is Deep South. (I have noticed that there is a large colony of native hillbillies, especially among the maintenance workers, taxi and bus drivers, and one taxi driver told me that the town was built around them.)

Oh, there is lots to tell about Oak Ridge. Upon arriving, I was immediately swept into the group of "professional wives." The women were extremely cordial and cooperative and very curious about newcomers. They live very well. If you "belong," have a car and telephone, live in one of the "permanent" houses, living here is pretty ideal. Household help is available—there is an employment agency—and baby-sitters are available. And believe me, there are plenty of babies to sit for. I understand that a good source for sitters is among single people living in dormitories, who are eager for a chance to be in homelike surroundings and perhaps have an opportunity to play a piano, have a home-cooked meal, or just read or study. There are also many husbands and wives (mostly Army) who must live apart because of peculiar housing conditions, and they welcome an opportunity to be together. I imagine one can easily forget any of the unpleasant aspects here—such as the Hooverville aspect, segregation, Army control—because you can become absorbed in your own social circle and be quite isolated from general life here.

As an example of their generosity, the day our furniture arrived, I sent out an SOS, and within fifteen minutes one woman offered to act as chauffeur for any of our needs, another volunteered to act as nursemaid to Irene and still another marketed for us. The neighbor next door (a perfect stranger) came over and invited us to use her phone at any time. She said she goes to work, but leaves her door open all the time and I should walk in. I was surprised to learn that most people never lock their doors.

There is every possible activity to meet with almost any hobby. But I am told that the Army did frown on any public meeting suggesting political action, and discouraged any attempts at formation of such groups.

I must tell you about the recently formed organization, though. A small group of alert scientists' wives decided it was time to come "out of the kitchen" and make themselves heard on the subject of atomic energy. I attended their third meeting last night, and the group had swelled to about sixty women. They intend to be partly auxiliary to the men's group, and also to act as an independent group for action, control, and education on atomic energy. I was terribly excited about their program and the number of intelligent and capable women, and the serious efforts that were made to translate talk into action. I intend to devote as much time to it as I can spare, and have volunteered to act on the publicity committee.

Unpacking our furniture with some thirty cartons was quite an adventure. Button, button, who's got the can opener? We've just about dug out, now, and even managed to wangle a telephone. Just call Oak Ridge 5-1169!

Well, Margaret, I haven't begun to tell you about this place. It's tremendous. And, by the way, I like it a lot. Although Oak Ridge is utterly different, I can't believe we are so far from home. We get WQXR—a great comfort but we do miss good news coverage.

Dick says, "Hello."

> Best to Gregory and Catherine.
> [*sig*] Thelma

P.S. There is an excellent and well-stocked library, including a couple of books by M. Mead.

Over thirty years have elapsed since my last letter to Margaret Mead. One day in 1980, I mused that it might be an interesting exercise to seek out some of the Oak Ridge pioneers and compare thoughts on those early days—which seemed so long ago. I made a list of questions bearing on what I had written. Then I chose Charmian and Waldo Cohn for my first interview for several reasons. They had been among the first settlers and were representative of many other scientists of their period. They had been in the vanguard—with other leading citizens—in promoting numerous endeavors to enrich the life of the city, and were still carrying on. I felt, too, that their comments would be accurate and objective. They were cooperative. I was encouraged to go further with my tentative ideas and to continue my probing.

Here is some of what the Cohns told me on Jan. 10, 1980:

Before Oak Ridge could be started, about a thousand residents occupying the area had to be evacuated. It was a difficult time for them—uprooting is usually a traumatic period. In this case, it was compounded by the fact that the reasons for their removal necessarily had to be vague; but it was the only way it could be done because of the secrecy, urgency, and the utmost seriousness of the war situation. The upheaval was accepted by some, others were suspicious and, perhaps, hostile; but all of them were removed and preparations for an ambitious city and project unlike anything that had ever existed in this country (or anywhere else in the world) were started in 1942.

Waldo arrived in 1943 and lived alone in a dorm for two weeks. He was to send for Charmian and son, Marc, as soon as their house was available. He was lonely (albeit excited about the work on the project), and couldn't stand life in the dorm. He called Charmian to come and said he would manage to find a place for them to stay.

A friendly couple with two children invited them to share their three-bedroom house. They, plus the three-and-a-half Cohns (Charmian was pregnant), literally camped together, sleeping on cots, sharing household chores and hardships of the primitive conditions of the city. The Cohns literally watched their house going up in rapid stages—assembly-line production—and moved in when it was completed, about a month later.

Most of the scientists came from universities—many got leaves of absence in cooperation with the war effort. Some called for one or more of their graduate students to come and work under them. Half of the scientists—average age in the twenties—were unmarried and lived in dorms. The Cohns considered themselves one of the oldest couples. He was 33, and she was 29 years old. There were a considerable number of infants and very young children. (Oak Ridge was probably the city with the youngest population in the country.) The scientists arrived—not all at once—as work progressed and more were needed and more housing became available. The city rapidly outgrew its projected few thousand persons. At its height, the end of the war in 1945, it had a population of 75,000.

In order to attract the scientists, the government had to pay higher salaries to compensate for the isolation and primitive conditions then existing. However, the pay was not the "bait" in most cases. Scientists earnestly wanted to be involved in the war effort, and were enthusiastic and stimulated by the challenge—all this, in spite of winter mud, summer dust, unpaved roads and scarcity of rationed gas. Few had cars, but bus service was good. There was only one cafeteria where all single people had to eat, as there were no cooking facilities in the dorms. The food was monotonous and far from what they were accustomed to. There were constant complaints, but no other places were ready at first.

In describing her first reactions, Charmian said that she was not dismayed by the gates, passes, the fact that the city was controlled by the Army, or the drastic changes in lifestyle that the undeveloped conditions brought on. She sensed that most important war work was going on, even though neither she nor any of the other wives—except those involved in the laboratories—knew what the actual work was. She was proud to be a part of the war effort and felt like a pioneer, as did most of the newcomers.

There was a general feeling of excitement and challenge. In a sense, she felt protected by the "gates." There was no household help, but there was a diaper service and a communal laundry.

Their first friendships were with those they already knew, mostly people in the lab where Waldo worked. Charmian rarely left Oak Ridge, as roads to surrounding cities were bad or nonexistent, and the cities did not have many attractions for them anyway. There was food and gas rationing, but most of the necessities were obtainable. Living was very casual—there was no feeling of having to "keep up with the Joneses," as most of the people felt they were "all in the same boat." This attitude resulted in lots of informal parties and home entertaining. It was customary for guests to leave their shoes at the door if muddy from a recent rain, which averaged four or five inches a month.

Baby-sitters were no problem. Single people were eager to escape the dorms and spend an evening in a "real" home. One soldier, after baby-sitting a few times, timidly asked a favor. He wondered if, after the Cohn children were asleep (by then there were two), he might have permission to take a bath! He hadn't had one in two years—only showers in a barracks. Thereafter, whenever he came to sit, it was understood he would have his bath.

Another tale of coming to Oak Ridge and the subsequent adjustments came from Cy and Rose Feldman. Cy begins their account:

> In September 1944 the plants at Oak Ridge were about to open, and although they were partly staffed with civilian engineers and scientists, they needed many more. So they went through the Army training camps and pulled out all the engineers, chemists, and physicists who had had two years of experience after their bachelor degrees, which exactly fit me at the time.
>
> I was in infantry basic training down at Fort Wheeler, Macon, Ga., and they simply sent Major Edgar Murphy and a personnel man. They toured the camps and interviewed people who met those qualifications. Then we were notified a little later that we would have to leave for an unknown destination. We left camp at 2 in the morning and got on a train with sealed orders, which we opened on the train. What did they say, but "get off at Knoxville." We were met by an Army truck which took us to Oak Ridge.
>
> Then all of the soldiers who were taken into Oak Ridge had to wait for several weeks there while their security clearances were checked by the FBI. I forget what we were doing during the time—probably push-ups—but eventually we were placed in positions in the plants right beside the civilians.

Rose Feldman joins in the story:

> We were married and already had a child almost a year old. After Cy went into the Army, we had a little apartment in Washington. When Cy left for Oak Ridge, I went home to stay with my family in Philadelphia—we're both from there and had met at the University of Pennsylvania.
>
> In Oak Ridge, the GIs lived in barracks, although they had no mess hall or anything. They ate in the cafeteria. There was no extra housing and the GIs were absolutely last on the list. If they could find a place to live, their families were allowed in—provided [their wives] were employed. Baby-sitting facilities were not so great, so it was going to be very difficult for me to come with a one-year-old child; although I had a degree in chemistry from the University of Pennsylvania and they could have used me.
>
> GI wives were permitted to come for three-day visits and stay at the Guest House. The husbands didn't have to be in the barracks those nights, so we had three days. But then I was supposed to leave. I remember he got a three-day pass for me. It was October, and it was beautiful. It's the prettiest time of year here anyway. But there was a civilian family named Fairbanks with two children—a boy and a girl—and they were entitled to a D house (three bedrooms). They rented out one of their bedrooms for short periods to GI couples, but for no more than a week at a time. I heard about it from a

Mexican boy named Mario Castillo, who was also in the Army. So I got to stay at the Fairbanks' house an extra week and after ten days, I went home.

During the week that I was there that October, I had answered several ads in the paper for places to live. I remember going to a flattop somewhere in East Village, which was teeming with flattops. One woman, whose husband was a construction man, had a broken leg. She had tripped going out to the sanitary facilities at night. The husband had to be out of the house by 6 A.M., and she wanted me to come and take care of her, fix her husband a big breakfast every morning, and keep the baby quiet all day because he worked weird hours and had to sleep. And we could pay them just $25 a month for the room.

Another family had a two-bedroom flattop. (If you remember, they were 24-feet square.) This was a mountain family with seven children, and they had a Warm Morning heater in the middle of the room. They had never had so much space in their whole lives. The whole family slept in that room and they rented out both their bedrooms to GI couples. That was the general pattern of ads we answered.

Ruth Carey and other people helped Cy look for a place to live and found a family with two little boys and a three-bedroom house. Two children of the same sex in a family entitled them to only a two-bedroom house, but there was a lot of finagling then. You claimed a grandmother who was living with you or something, so you got an extra room. They rented out that bedroom to us for $25 a month furnished. It had a bed that must have been from 1875 that had a mattress in two sections. I had never seen one of these before, but Cy's mother told me they used to be common around the turn of the century. It had one square section and one narrow section so that you could shift the narrow one and it wore the mattress evenly, if you were going to keep it a hundred years. We had a plywood chest that they had in the flattops, which we still have, a card table, which I guess was made out of an orange crate. It was very rough and just painted over. And that was our furniture. We paid $25 a month for that, and the whole house rented for $53.50 or $57.50 a month.

The wife hated housework and hated cooking—you know, it was wartime and there was rationing and shortages. Our arrangement was that we split the household expense money half and half. Then we took turns cooking. We each cooked for two weeks, and the one who cooked did all the marketing, prepared menus and meals, and cleaned up after dinner. But for breakfast and lunch, the cook of the week just had to have the food on hand. We'd get our own breakfast and lunch.

Our landlady felt that we would be better off if two families with very different backgrounds did not eat at the same table, and if we kept our distance socially. And I think she was really right. They ate in the kitchen, where there was a table, and we had the little card table that we could use either in the combination living-dining room or in our own room, which we did very often. In the evenings we had use of the kitchen, and we could shut the door of our room where the baby was asleep and listen to the radio or write letters. Occasionally, we'd go out, and we'd baby-sit for each other. We were free to have company and to use the whole house. It worked out quite well, really. We parted friends.

Ida Coveyou, one of the new brides, contributes an account of young love in a young city:

We were married in Chicago in September 1943, and my husband left immediately for Oak Ridge. By December, he thought he had some housing. We were supposed to get what was called an E-1 apartment. These apartments were made of cemesto, and two middle apartments had a lower and upperfloor—each with two bedrooms—and at each end were one-bedroom apartments.

But ours—a one-room apartment—was not quite finished. My husband walked by it every day, and it looked as if the building was going up very fast. But, when you were an individual waiting for your house to be finished in Oak Ridge, you had to get used to what happens in mass housing. First, you waited for the plumbing or the roof or something else. It looked as it it were never going to get done. So my husband said, "How about coming down anyway? We'll probably get faster progress if you get here."

So I came on December 7 (who can forget that date?), moved into the Guest House, and started right in to work. Bob had to stay in a dormitory, since the Guest House was crowded. The top floor of the Guest House had a common room with some twenty to forty beds. The girl whose bed was touching mine and the girl next to her were young sisters, 16 and 17, who had come from nearby cities to work as waitresses. They had gotten sick on the way down and went straight to bed. They never got up for three days to eat or do anything. I was scared. "What could they have?"

How can you tell what is wrong when no one is checking on two kids this young, who were down and sick in bed? I was worried, so I went straight to the doctor at the plant. The doctor also was concerned. He went right out to the Guest House that same day. When I got back, the girls were feeling better. They got up, dressed, went home, and never came back. They had had enough of Oak Ridge!

All the housing was assigned from the plant where you worked, and when it looked as if I might stay in that common room and Bob might stay in the dormitory (because we didn't know when that apartment was going to be finished), we made a daily practice of eating with the housing manager. We all ate in the big cafeteria, and we'd look around to see where he was sitting, join him and say, "What's happening?" He got awfully tired of seeing us every day at meals, and you'd be surprised how fast he found some other housing for us.

We got a two-room, furnished efficiency apartment. It had a combined living room and kitchen with a screen to hide the kitchen whenever we wanted to. It was small, and the refrigerator was tiny. It was satisfactory enough for the purpose at that time. I still remember the furnishings and coming home one day. In great excitement I said to my husband, "They've built in an ironing board!" And he said, "Hey, wait, that's our dining-room table!"

Another time I did my usual weekly marketing on the way home. Coming out with two bags loaded with groceries, there was a sudden downpour. It was coming down so hard it soaked the thin bags, and all the groceries rolled out in the mud. When you've got nothing to put them in, it's awkward!

Eight days after I first wrote to Margaret Mead, she replied:

New York City
March 21, 1946

Dear Thelma,

It was grand to get your letter and know that you were practically dug in— and out of your cartons. I know the general state—forty boxes and a lost packing list. The other thing that can happen—with boxes but not cartons— mercifully—is to lose all your keys.

The things that interested me most in your letter—rather naturally!—was the fine state of sitters, and the way in which "sitting" has become a way of attaining social life for the dormitory dweller. There have been various developments like that—I remember out in Topeka it was a way in which high school girls whose families lived in close quarters—could see their boy-friends. Then there was a scandal in Bronxville because a Sarah Lawrence girl sitter had another girl from Sarah Lawrence—of a different race—over to spend the evening with her—although the same girl would have been a perfectly acceptable primary sitter. I suppose husbands become secondary sitters, more social than the sitter? Quite a little folklore might develop about it.

Then I was interested in the unlocked doors and the way people can run in and out of each other's houses. Of course that happens on certain kinds of ships—all one class and a high state of being in a closed-off secure world. It might be due to the fact that no one could get out of town—rather the way England is supposed to have less crime because it is so hard to get off the island. Of course there might be another explanation—people seeking out areas of ease as a sort of counterpoint to areas of strain. Or it may just be that it's like any Southern town. I would make a guess that doors aren't locked much in the South, partly because there are usually servants about—yard boys, nurse maids, etc.

Cathy's[2] two contributions this week: (1) She and I came into the Museum on Saturday ahead of opening time, and some irate little boys shouted, "It doesn't open until 10." Cathy turned to me and remarked, "They don't know we work here." (2) She had got into a row with the daughter of an artist, and when questioned as to what the other child had done, she said, "She said she didn't like our job." I asked, "What job?" "Being scientists!"

Gregory sends his best to you both,

Yours,
[sig] Margaret

In addition to the interviews, some of the material in this book came from tapings of a seminar at the Children's Museum of Oak Ridge in 1980. Helen Jernigan was moderator of a panel on "The Way It Was in Oak Ridge." Three

---

[2]Dr. Mary Catherine Bateson Kassarjian, Margaret's daughter.

others I shall quote later—Kathryn Cantrell, the late Julia Moore and Alice Lyman were part of the same group. The Learning Museum Program, lasting from January 8 to March 11, was called "An Appalachian Experience" and was funded by the National Endowment for the Humanities.

Helen also commented on the lack of locking up, which had intrigued Margaret:

> In the barracks, there were no keys on the doors. Men lived in one wing and women in the other. Nothing was ever stolen from me or anybody else I knew. The reason partly being, I suppose, the tight security of everybody who was here. Nobody who had a criminal record of any kind could work here.

Letter II

Oak Ridge, Tenn.
March 26, 1946

Dear Margaret,

I lost my red purse, and walked to town today to put an ad in the Oak Ridge Journal. This is the one paper (for adult consumption) that is published here and is a weekly. It is sent to all residents for free—and is controlled by the Army. What a funny little office. Looks like a scene from a one-act play, with all the personnel trying so hard to look their parts. One girl reporter with huge glasses, severe hairdo and mannish clothes was scowling at her typewriter, gnawing her fingernails.

Whenever I leave the house and wander about, I feel a little like giggling. I have that continuing sense of unreality, impermanence, and of being a spectator. Everything looks so temporary—almost like a movie set with cardboard dwellings or a plan of a city such as you might see in the Museum of Modern Art. There are about eight types of dwellings that are completely standardized, and I hope to get around to seeing them all. I think it would interest you.

The city is well-planned and has the good and bad aspects of any small town, except that everything seems intensified. One interesting aspect is the way completely heterogeneous people lead similar lives depending on their social status. Among the professional group, for instance, the social scale depends on the plant where the husband works. You are a Carbide wife, a TEC (Tennessee Eastman Corporation) wife or a Clinton [Engineer Works] wife. The latter is tops, and since Dick works there on pure research two days a week, I suppose I'm ⅖ tops. A further distinction is made by calling the wives by the husband's profession. So, I am a physicist. The avenues go in alphabetical order, and all the streets leading from an avenue start with the

23

same letter. The streets, in turn, are in alphabetical order after the first letter. In a short time it is very easy to find your way about. There are several residential sections. The houses are clustered together in groups of about fifteen on the ridges. There is a decent space around each house, and they seem to have been placed for a maximum of light—sort of catty-corner to each other. They are all painted white, and I still am never sure I am entering my own house unless I watch the number.

When you leave your house and go to one of the main centers, it feels like coming into a factory town from a suburb. The markets swarm with people. Mothers shop with their babies in their arms; the bus stations are crowded with workers, big shopping bags, high school kids, etc. I'm always so glad to get home with all our familiar things around.

Except that I sometimes feel we are living in a goldfish bowl. I would have to pull down six shades and two venetian blinds (as would everyone else in a B house) for any privacy in my living room. I have the feeling my neighbors would be hurt, if I did. And talking about neighbors, we have a young bride next door from Nowth Calina, who bounces in several times a day. She likes to "keep" for Irene. Not only that, she brings me fudge!

We were dying to escape the mess here one night last week, so I started tracking down some "sitters." I was advised to call the school for a list of youngsters. When I explained what I wanted to the teacher who answered the phone, she said she would be delighted to come. She lives in the "dorm." She was young and pretty, and remarked that she had almost forgotten what a home looked like. Some friends of ours have a wonderful setup. Five boys came together to "sit" and listen to their records. There is a lot of exchanging of husbands and wives.[1] Then there are families who don't bother with "sitters." At the movies that night, there were lots of very young children with their parents—including infants in their mothers' arms. A friend told me that she saw a woman waiting in line for a seat also holding a baby. Why don't the fathers hold 'em?

You made an analogy of O.R. (which, incidentally, has barbed wire all around the city) to a ship or an island. I sometimes have the feeling of a sanatorium—that we have been committed here. Also, when I went to get my badge, I felt as if I were going to prison. You know, we got temporary passes before we came, and they were valid for a specific period. We hadn't yet signed for the house when we went to get the passes exchanged for resident badges, and had to return after the lease was signed. They ask you routine questions, then you poke your head through a box to get your picture taken. A sign on the desk says, "If you don't like your picture, remember, we can't improve on nature." Irene laughed when she saw Dick's, but she turned her head away when I showed her mine.

Few residents have any urge to fix their grounds. I have heard many people say they don't feel like bothering because they don't know how long they will stay. Then, of course, no one owns his home. Pet boasts are screened porches

---

[1]What I meant, of course, was for baby-sitting purposes.

and fenced-in yards. Did I tell you that this place has millions of babies and
dogs?

All babies born here are registered as having O.R. as their birthplace.
During the war, because of the secrecy, the births were registered by a G.I.
Now there is a statistician here with two assistants helping him fill in back
records. I learned from a nurse that there are about the same amount of
illegitimate babies as most places. But I'd like to check that.

We hadn't noticed any graveyards, and I asked about it. There are two in
the "area" that were here before. Among those who died here, hardly any are
buried in O.R. Because there were proportionately few old people, the death
rate was very low. This is all talk, of course. It is very difficult to get any
statistics. In fact, you have to depend on the Knoxville papers for most of the
news on O.R.[2]

Knowing how rushed you are, I appreciated your prompt reply, and was
delighted to hear about the family. I shall not be formal, but write when I have
the urge. So don't feel obligated to answer every letter. I am sending you
some souvenirs.

> Regards from us,
> [sig] Thelma

While I was gathering interviews for this book in 1980, one of the Oak Ridge
Army obstetricians told me that there was such an overabundance of pregnant
women that the Army had to add more and more obstetricians to keep up with
the rate of births. One memorable and record evening, he said, babies started
tumbling out with the speed and regularity of an assembly line. He alone
delivered twelve babies within twelve hours!

Among my interviews was one with Bettie Levy, who spoke of many facets
of life as she found it in the Atomic City. Here are some of her impressions
upon arrival:

> Well, I moved into a dormitory in Oak Ridge in October '46, and by that
> time the town had been there for four years and the dormitories were in the
> last utter condition of dilapidation. It looked as if beer parties and pie-
> throwing had gone on in the room they gave me. It was not inspiring. In fact,
> living in a dormitory was not much fun. There were no kitchen facilities or
> anything. There was a group bathroom, if you want to dignify it by that name,
> which had running water—if you can call a "trickle" running water—and they
> had shower rooms, washrooms and toilet facilities. This was before the day of
> plastics. The women used glass shampoo bottles and the wood-slatted floors
> in the shower room were littered with broken glass all the time. You had just

---

[2]In the war years and long before they could admit there was such a place as Oak Ridge, the
Knoxville newspapers carried bowling scores from Oak Ridge leagues. League and team
names were equally unrevealing.

one nozzle—no spray. The shower sprays—if they had ever been there—had been stolen long before I got there.

It was primitive, like a summer camp that had been inhabited by degenerates. It wasn't very nice. The only nice thing was that I had a double room all to myself. I had requested a single room. But by that time, the crowds weren't as great and they happened to have a room with two beds. So I could have a visitor once in a while—same sex naturally.

Male guests were not allowed past the front desk. They had a woman who monitored whoever came in. So we would meet our dates at community recreation halls or at the homes of married friends.

In the spring of '47, some friends invited me to move into their D house and share the rent, because one of the girls had left and they were down to five people. The D houses had three bedrooms. In the early days, it seemed that the Government had built more D houses than it turned out were needed, as it was such a young community. Since only families with enough children were allowed to have them, not many were eligible for three-bedroom houses. At first, they rented out a number of these houses to twelve single people. They put two double-decker beds in a room and the three bedrooms would hold twelve men or twelve women. This was before I got there. They were called "temporary dormitories" and were occupied as soon as they were built, because there was an overflow in the other dormitories almost immediately.

After the war, with so many people leaving or terminated, a "temporary dormitory" could be rented to as few as six persons, and I lived in that D house until I was married to Henri later that year.

Henri was one of the first arrivals to Oak Ridge. He came from Cal Tech as a research physical chemist in September '43 and worked at X-10 lab. He also lived in a dormitory at first, for a couple of years.

I had joined a hiking club when I came to East Tennessee. I hadn't moved to Oak Ridge yet. But right after V-J Day, Henri finally had a day off. The scientists there had been working untold hours—eighty hours a week—tremendous amounts. He really hadn't dated or had any kind of recreation until then.

We met on his first day with the hiking club on the Appalachian Trail. We started dating and went together for about two years until we got married, as it turned out. Before that, the only time I went to Oak Ridge was to see my date. Henri would come to the guardhouse to meet my bus from Knoxville. He always got there on time with a pass for me. Even though he had a car, he had to conserve gas because of the rationing. He would take me to dinner, visit some friends, or we'd go to a concert of the Oak Ridge Symphony. That was the usual type of date. We sometimes went to a dance or to whatever else was going on. Then he took me back to the bus station in time to catch the bus home. There just wasn't enough gas to go gallivanting.

Henri told me that any time he got sick, which was rarely, he could always stay with a married couple and the wife would ply him with chicken soup. He spent so little time in the dormitory, he didn't even know what people did for recreation. He knows he just didn't have time for it. It was all work. For diversion on Sundays, they would watch blocks of cemesto houses being put up. But that's the way things were in those early days.

Henri's roommate was married. He was eager to get into a house right away and be reunited with his wife and baby. In fact all of the married men with small families (and/or more children on the way) wanted to get into houses as soon as they were built. Because of the housing requirements, they were always having to change how they laid out the dormitories. (Other dormitories were full of construction workers and technicians.) I think it was according to how much security clearance you had.

One day they decided that Henri's dormitory would have to be changed to women's quarters. They had to keep the sexes separate and apparently there was an overflow somewhere. The men were to be moved into another building. One of the "big shots" in the administration [who lived in the dorm] was due to move into his house in three days, and wasn't about to move twice. So he got whoever was in charge to change the order. They were already pulling out the urinals in the restroom, and the next thing Henri knew when he came back, they were putting the urinals back in.

The men kept moving all the time. Henri asked for a single room, which he got. Then he moved in with a young couple.[3] They finally had been able to wangle a two-bedroom efficiency apartment, provided that they would share it. They invited Henri to be their roomer, and in that way they could swing the rent and it would be more pleasant. An added bonus to the couple was the fact that Henri had a higher position and had to be on call. He therefore was able to requisition a telephone! So it was a symbiotic relationship.

In September 1947 Henri and I decided to get married and set the date for November 1. We had to figure out a way for all the relatives to be notified, and get passes and accommodations for them. These things were not easy right after the war. Henri had already taken his vacation that year, such as it was (involving family), and was not able to get any more time. But his supervisor said, "You won't be any good to us. Why don't you just disappear for a week?" So we did, and when we got back, there still wasn't any housing for us. We stayed at the Guest House (now the Alexander Hotel) for another week while Henri looked frantically for something for us to live in.

One place the housing office found for us was the Monticello Apartments in the Jefferson Center area. Those awful things! We walked in and looked at the apartment, and I said, "If that is what it takes, 'Good-bye.' " Back at the Guest House, we read that the manager of the Oak Ridge swimming pool had dropped dead of a heart attack. We looked up his address, a K apartment off West Outer Drive. We drove up there immediately and peeked in the windows. It was a one-bedroom apartment, and it was reasonable. Henri rushed to the housing office and said, "How about apartment number so and so on Wade Lane?" She looked it up and said, "Yes, that is available and you are eligible for it."

We lived in that apartment until our first child, Janny, was born in 1949. By

---

[3]Ida and Bob Coveyou.

then, things were really calming down. Many families were moving away—especially the huge construction crews—and the town was getting a little smaller. People were starting to want to live a little better, and the absolutely nicest kind of a three-bedroom house was the F house. One of the big shots who had been living in a rather small, three-bedroom C house was moving into an F house and I knew he was. So again, I said to Henri, "Since we are going to move from our apartment, why move into a two-bedroom house when you are eligible for a C house?" We did not have any illusions of grandeur and didn't want a D or F house, which would have been fancier. The moment we heard the S _____'s were leaving, Henri put in for their house.

We are still living there. We have remodeled it twice and sometimes I think, "Well, maybe we should have gone ahead and moved twice." Of course, we could have waited and gotten a D or F, but I am happy with where we live. When the houses were put up for sale, there was not much difference in the price. The average price was from about $3,000 to $8,000. Even though they were made of some heavy-duty cardboard, the price was certainly reasonable for what we got. We have put in many times more than what we gave for it in remodeling the way we did; we did this not with an eye to sales value, but with the way it fitted our needs. I suppose we could get out of it at least what we have put into it—with these inflated prices today.

Our social life revolved almost entirely about the scientific group. There weren't many other people that I can think of. (Of course, there were the AEC managerial people and there were service personnel from all the stores, etc.) But the scientists were all young together—their children were all born about the same time. We also kept our hiking friends from Knoxville, my friends from TVA, and went to the Knoxville Symphony. Then it got to be so hard to get into Knoxville, it became largely the scientists and their families with whom we had social contact.

On the surface, it appeared that everybody got housing not according to personal wealth or salaries, but according to needs and requirements. Although the rules were bent a little for some top people in key positions whose feelings needed to be soothed in order to keep them working. Still, the differences were not great. There was a sort of leveling out because of the urgency of the work, wartime rationing, no gas (things that people could not do in common—like driving around), boardwalks, and the mud. Everybody dressed informally.

Charmian Cohn also applauded the casualness of Oak Ridge life. "Hardly anyone tried to 'outdo' in home decoration, and all enjoyed the informality." And she and her husband, Waldo, pointed out that house maintenance included free electricity and coal, by which all houses were heated. Very few of the residents had ever stoked a furnace before! There was regular—sometimes too regular—maintenance such as painting and repairs performed by crews which appeared at any hour. The Army also provided topsoil for those who desired lawns and gardens. Considering the pressure the Army was under to get Oak Ridge ready, amazing care was taken to preserve trees, to respect the contours of the hills and ridges, and to see that placement of the houses ensured privacy and pleasant views. All this was done by the firm of Skidmore, Owings & Merrill's community division, to which the Army had entrusted the city design. Rents were extremely low, more so considering all the services. They even tried for variety in the cemesto houses, by building half as mirror images.

Kathryn Cantrell, who joined her husband in Oak Ridge in 1944, had a friend who took a different view of the town's housing, seeing in it the sameness that had also impressed me. Mrs. Cantrell (at the children's museum seminar) had this to say about her friend Virginia, who came to Oak Ridge the same year that she did:

> As the family had a boy and a girl, they were eligible for a three-bedroom house. When her husband came to pick them up and take them to Oak Ridge, he described the house and she could not understand a house with just one door. But when they got there, they were very pleased with the accommodations—so much so that they rented a room to a young GI and his wife. One day Virginia's little boy was sitting on the steps next door, and she wondered why he was sitting over there so long. She called for him to come home, but he said, "I *am* home."
>
> The houses were all alike, Mrs. Cantrell added, and were all painted the same color. It was very hard to find your way home in those days.

Ida, too, praised the informality of the early days, despite her ordeal with the dissolving grocery bags:

> But there were so many pleasant and just plain fun things.
>
> Rationing was in at that time and we used to have an enormous amount of company. I can't believe it when I think back—all the company almost every night. Most of them were from the lab and lived in dormitories. They were awfully tired of eating out and it didn't take much to entertain them—they had the [food rationing] stamps anyway. When we invited them over, we all cooked together. The place was small, but it didn't make any difference. It was like a college group. You didn't have to show off or demonstrate anything. Anyone who could make something special would go ahead and make it. We either played chess or other games or talked or whatever. There were always people around to do things with. If you had to wash your hair or your clothes, you did it. There were good opportunities for getting together with people from totally different cultures and class backgrounds—religious and ethnic.
>
> When we first came, most of us ate breakfast in the big Central Hall cafeteria, and we saw everybody there. Then we took buses out to the lab or hitchhiked our way there. We got acquainted with a lot of people that way. There wasn't any question about it, we did work hard. This was not a period to

waste time. But it was such an easy atmosphere. I never knew who was a world-famous scientist or not, because I shared offices with scientists who didn't tell me they were world-famous. Later, when I began to read a little more physics and saw many of their names quoted, I realized whom I had shared offices with.

But really, we were so busy and so involved with ourselves. After all, so many of us had just married and were working on new jobs. We had to figure what to do about common things like food and making your own arrangements. Even though it was quite different from Chicago, it didn't bother me at all. It was just fun—like going off on a vacation in a different country where you knew it would be different. When you go on vacation, you don't want to replace your everyday life and comforts. You don't miss the paved streets and facilities. You want it to be different.

It was also a time of having so many friends. For those of us who didn't have phones, life was even more informal. One very prominent woman told me much later that one morning she didn't get dressed as early as usual and somebody came over around 8:30. They sat down and had coffee. Before that person left at 8:50, someone else just came by with some news and they sat down and had coffee. At 9:15 she still wasn't dressed and a third friend dropped in. By the time her husband came home at 5, she was still in her bedclothes, drinking coffee with yet another friend.

But it was that kind of thing. We all had the same kind of housing. It wasn't the place or the time to show off the fancy things you had. Many years later, I heard about a Belgian family who had an elaborate chandelier. They worried about what to do with something so elegant in a cemesto house.

We had places to go, such as the Ridge Rec Hall, where we'd go to play ping-pong or square dance. Everyone was very friendly and you could always find somebody to play with.

In her next and following letters, Margaret Mead showed her continuing interest in the social makeup of Oak Ridge, the homology and diversity of which have been shown in some of the preceding interviews and will be embellished later.

New York City
April 2, 1946

Dear Thelma,

I've been down with malaria, which explains my long delay in writing. I enjoyed the papers you sent and think the number of the Oak Leaf[4] particularly good. Do you suppose that full use is being made of it by the Atomic Information center in Washington? If I had some idea what had been done already I might take the matter up with them. It ought to be reproduced in

---

[4]"Oak Leaves" (not "Oak Leaf") was a regular column in the *Oak Ridge Journal*.

educational journals, in youth-serving organization journals, etc. I have written for more copies but have not received an answer yet.

I was interested in your account of the different layers of society in OR and I wonder how differently they feel about the whole problem. It could be that there were strongly contrasting attitudes in different sharply marked off areas of town or I suppose the high school and general atmosphere might have smoothed those differences out. Perhaps they would show up in the schools—particularly in junior high school, as I suppose many of the students from the poorer areas never reach high school. But it would be good to know what determines attitudes—a trailer, a poor meagre background, or what is sometimes called "group atmosphere." How widely is the town paper read, for instance?

The world seems to be very full of relevant movie scripts at present, and Gregory spends a lot of time writing critiques of them. He has now got a Guggenheim and that plus his series of lectures at the New School[5] next year loom on the horizon and compete with the movie scripts.

Your days sound checkered—but interesting. At present I am experiencing the horrors of deafness—but only from quinine.

Yours,
[sig] Margaret

The first impact of Oak Ridge on the surrounding area was more physical than cultural, or so were the observations of Ann Wachter, whose parents lived nearby. She had this to say in 1982:

In 1942, I was a student of sociology at the University of Tennessee in Knoxville. One Friday I took the bus from there to spend the weekend with my parents in Oakdale, Tennessee, where I grew up. I noticed vaguely that the bus was fuller than usual between Clinton and Oliver Springs and that it stopped unexpectedly at a place that seemed out of nowhere. A man in Army uniform got on, stood by the door in the front of the bus, and the bus went on.

No one paid much attention, but before long the bus stopped again and a couple of men wearing strange caps got off at an unfamiliar place after showing something to the man in uniform. While that was happening, I looked out of the window and there in an empty field were loads and loads of bathtubs!

I thought, "What in the world!"

I couldn't contain my curiosity any longer so I asked the person next to me, "Do you know what all this is?"

I got the explanation that some big secret Government project was going on out there. Because the other person was a stranger, I didn't pursue the

---

[5]The New School for Social Research started in New York in 1930. It listed professionals in all disciplines and gave courses in many fields.

matter. The bus continued on to Oliver Springs and the uniformed man got off. When I got home, I asked my father, "What is happening between Clinton and Robertsville?"

He said he knew that it was a closely guarded area, that anyone who wanted a job could get one, and that a couple of families from around there had had to move out because of it.

At that time in Clinton, about ten miles from Oak Ridge, there were about six hundred homes—not a very large population. Suddenly in 1943, there were several thousand people looking for housing and parking space—for any place to live while they were working at this "closely guarded" place. Houses, rooms, garages, barns—even chicken houses—were shifted for rooming space. Trailers and tents sprang up. Here were people encroaching on a small town with such speed and in such numbers that neither the newcomers nor the old-timers had enough water, electric power, postal or telephone services, sewage, educational, recreational or religious facilities; and Clinton's little streets were choked with traffic. Many of these first newcomers were construction people from small Appalachian towns.

The "early people" shock was not so much due to the invasion by people of divergent cultures, but, very likely, because of the sudden and vast influx of people with their accompanying demands. The early history and growth of Oak Ridge was so swift, dramatic and incomprehensible that the bewildering effect on the surrounding towns is understandable. The advent of this mystifying city fostered many wild tales in the region about what was "going on" in THAT place.

Letter III

Oak Ridge, Tenn.
April 8, 1946

Dear Margaret,

Today I went exploring, and by simply taking the No. 9 bus, I was transported to Inferno. This bus is labeled HUTMENTS.

A few other white people got on and filled the front few seats. I sat near the rear, and a colored woman said someone had saved me a seat in the front, but I said it didn't matter where I sat. It was a long ride to the other end of town and the houses and neighborhoods got worse and worse until you cross the railroad track, and, appropriately, there is the camp. That is what it is called.

The first things you see are signs saying NO LOAFERS ALLOWED. It seemed as if there were about a thousand of these fifteen-foot-square huts with cone-shaped tops, all painted a deadly olive drab, and arranged compactly in a three-quarter circle and rising up—stadium fashion.

I got to talking to Beulah, who was the first settler there, four years ago. She comes from Chattanooga, where her husband and son live; and while she would prefer living home, she says she makes more money in the camp and is staying until her son graduates from Tuskegee next year. He is studying doctoring. Then she is going to give him fifty dollars and turn him loose.

On the right side are the men's huts, and opposite—behind the pen—are the women's. The pen is a high wooden fence and is supposed to keep the men out. That's what Beulah said.

There are no sinks or toilets in the huts, but several real nice ones that everybody uses. There is a large recreation hall where they have movies a few nights a week and those who are not at work sort of hang around during the day. Then there is a dance hall, but they don't hold dances more than once a week, because some people get too drunk.

33

There are no markets, shops, drug stores or anything except a barber shop in the camp. They have to take a bus to the nearest stores. Married folks with children live just on the other side of the tracks in "Victory Cottages," in appearance about twice the size of the huts, and all are a dirty white. All of the colored children go to school in Clinton, which is the next town and I think about twelve miles away. They are taken by bus. There is a loudspeaker which is heard all over the camp for communication and messages. Then I had to leave, but I promised Beulah I'd come again. I liked her.

We went to the Symphony last week, and it was unique. Anyone coming to O.R. who plays an instrument is nabbed. We felt obligated to go, because we knew a few people in the orchestra. The audience showed remarkable restraint. Our sitter who teaches in elementary school chatted with us while waiting for the bus. She mentioned that there is a very nice class of children in her school. They come from "permanent" homes. The type of children in the schools depend on its locality, the trailer section being very poor. (Incidentally, there is a U.S. Post Office there called the Trailer City Branch.)

I am always surprised at the way rumors get around in here—a city so tremendous and widely dispersed. I have been getting nasty reports about a section called Middletown (not to be confused with the book). There is a neighborhood just before you get to the Hutments, and it is supposed to house the "white trash." They "say" there's lots of loose living, brawls, even a few murders, and also a dope ring was discovered there. Well, take rumors for what they are.

But what interests me is the way O.R. is blocked out. Everything has its place and everything seems to be there. The blocks are clear-cut and nothing overlaps.

There are no special parks or playground areas, except at the schools and nursery schools (two high schools, eleven elementary schools and several nurseries). So if you want company for yourself or child, you visit or have visitors.

I asked another acquaintance, who was one of the first settlers here, about the unlocked doors. They haven't used their key in years. There are so many officials on the area with pass keys that they realized it didn't make any difference if they did or didn't lock their doors. Anybody entering a house with a pass key was supposed to be escorted—but, they wondered. Do you know that there is no jail in O.R.? The nearest one is in Clinton. Also, there are no bells on the doors.

Only three more days left to pay the poll tax! We are not eligible to vote, but imagine us having to pay a tax when we *can* vote. According to the O.R. Journal, approximately 250 persons have paid the tax here at the time the paper went to press. I have gathered that there is very little publicity or information as to the procedure on voting. Also, a lot of red tape, and you can't vote in O.R. proper anyway, but in one of the nearby towns.

Oh yes, our guest towels are up, and this is the setup. We have two studio couches in our living room. We can't promise you and/or Gregory much privacy, but if you like "roughing" it, let us know. It would be fun for us.

Regards from Dick.

[sig] Thelma

Charmian and Waldo Cohn recalled segregation in Oak Ridge's early days:

Many people were upset by it and some complained. The Army's response was to the effect that their job, with the war constantly in mind, was to get the city functioning with as little friction as possible; they were not embarked on a sociological experiment. Northerners, particularly, were more disturbed by the segregation aspect, but understood what the Southern tradition was at that time. All realized that their war work was the first priority.

Ida, who had come from Chicago, also was troubled by segregation:

In the late forties, we were gradually struck by the distinctions between blacks and the whites. Black children simply were not seen in the white community. We learned that the men and women lived separately; families could not live under one roof. Most of us didn't know much about the situation, but there were some people at the lab who were concerned about health, including Negro health, and felt it was lacking a lot.

We also learned that most of the Negroes who had come to Oak Ridge had been hired from the streets of Mississippi and Alabama. They would be hanging around on a street corner. If someone wanted ten people to work, he hired them there. Many of these people couldn't read or write. All they knew was that they were being taken to a place called Oak Ridge. They didn't know where it was or how long it would be or even how they would get back. It was just a place to have a job.

Around 1945, Mr. and Mrs. Robert Officer were invited to come here and set up a school[1] for black children. They ran the school up to the eighth grade. Bob and I became acquainted with Mrs. Officer and talked to her quite a lot about the situation. Later, others became involved. Mrs. Officer, the principal, was a very able, competent and modest woman, and it hurt her a lot that the same children who went to school—good kids—stopped going to school after the eighth grade because they would not go to Knoxville where they were supposed to continue. They did not want to have to take the regular bus and stay in the back of it. She told us that the children who had finished the eighth grade were just sitting around at the old school. (A ninth grade was added later—partly because of all these students.)

---

[1]When Scarboro Elementary School was founded in 1946 for the Negro children in that community, Mrs. Arizona Officer was hired by the school administration as principal. Her husband, Robert, was employed as a teacher at the same time. Mrs. Officer had graduated from Morristown College, a small Negro institution in a town some forty miles northeast of Knoxville, Tennessee. As there were no facilities there for higher education for Negroes, the school administration paid her expenses to go to Columbia University.

In 1951, the Scarboro Student Aid Committee was organized to encourage black students to enter college. Mrs. Officer was actively engaged, with the committee, in providing some financial assistance, counseling and help to the prospective college students.

Bob and I thought that if these kids were not going to school anyway, then maybe we could help them. Northerners and Southerners, too, felt concerned about these children. Bob spoke to the Feltons[2] about it and they suggested talking to Mrs. Officer.

Mrs. Officer was in favor it it. When Bob began to sound people out, he found that this was a very appealing idea at the time. He got together Ph.D.s who said they were willing to teach, and most of the high school subjects could be covered. Jan Felton's advice was that we shouldn't just go ahead and teach as volunteers but rather talk to the school administrators.

We sat down and discussed who should meet with the superintendent of the Knoxville schools. The group of five—including scientists, a woman, an academic person—prepared themselves carefully. They listed arguments so they would have ready answers. Then they wrote in advance for an appointment with the superintendent and explained why they wanted to talk to him. He made an appointment quickly.

When they met, he said, "I'm turning you over to my assistant who is well versed in the matter." The assistant, who later became superintendent, was a Southerner who was extremely interested. He said that to run a school at all, you could not chance having only volunteers with the possibility of their leaving the next year with none to replace them.

The state Department of Education agreed to back the school. Two-and-a-half teachers were hired who would teach the basic subjects. This would keep the school going continuously; and whoever else wished to volunteer would be fine, since the school probably would not have a great many children to start with. So, actually, there was no argument.

We started with about ten children, including some who had been going to high school in Knoxville. As we were ending the first year, we had three graduates who had no idea what they were going to do. So we made arrangements to take them to Nashville. Two of the students enrolled in college there. I'm not sure where the third went after graduation. Three juniors all went to college, too. And these were the first black children from Oak Ridge who began work in biology and other scientific capacities. They later were some of the early professional Scarboro people; and some of these students, who are now parents, are active and knowledgeable citizens in the community and the city.

Among those I talked to in 1980 were two black women, Tommy Stevens and Lavada Chisholm, who told in impromptu interviews of their lives before

---

[2]Dr. Jean Felton, head of the Health Division of Oak Ridge National Laboratory, and his wife Jan made one of the earliest community volunteers' contacts between white and black Oak Ridgers when they organized a Health Clinic for Scarboro residents in 1946. Vaccinations and health information were offered.

Jan was deeply involved in starting the Scarboro Day Care Center in 1962. Members from the white churches volunteered their services by taking care of the children of working mothers in Scarboro. The center was under the direction of Mrs. Melvin Phillips, a black. The Center still is in operation on an integrated basis.

segregation began to crumble, and their resentment at the slowness of the process. They spoke to me singly and at times in counterpoint. Here is what they had to say:

Tommy: When I first came to Oak Ridge, I lived in what they called the Hutment area. That is the area that is now Woodland—the part of Woodland that's on the way to Knoxville. We lived there with wood sidewalks and muddy streets. The Hutments were like tepee wooden houses. I lived with my aunt.

At that time I was, let me see, still in elementary school—Scarboro Elementary School—so I must have been in the fifth or sixth grade, which would have made me eleven or twelve years old. The Scarboro School at that time was all black. We weren't allowed to go to school in Oak Ridge. We had buses that came out and picked us up, and we were bused past the elementary schools of Oak Ridge to this makeshift school. It wasn't really makeshift, it was a lovely school; and we were well educated, because we had a ratio of about three or four children in a class and we got a lot of attention. Because, with the city being so secretive and everything, they had to be very careful about the teachers and (some of them) were very well-qualified to teach. (The old Scarboro School building is now part of the Oak Ridge Associated Universities.)

The part of the Hutment area where I lived was for single women only—my aunt was not married. I'd come down and stay with her at intervals. Eventually, I just stayed. I think maybe some of the rules were a bit lighter— or weren't as strictly enforced—in the black area. I imagine there was a lot of outlawing done all over the city, but it seemed much higher here. Anyway, these wooden huts were square, and there was a bed in each corner. In the center of the floor was a coal heater that heated up the whole Hutment. The area had a community cafeteria and bathhouse, and in the morning, everybody made a mad dash to the bathhouse and a mad dash to the cafeteria and then a mad dash to the bus stop to go to school or work.

My aunt was a maid and she worked for the Management Service people. She had to clean the Hutments, and she did that until the change came about. The women were supposed to be separated from the men, but sometimes you couldn't tell. In the women's areas, the women fired the furnaces in the Hutments and the bathhouses to keep the water warm, and the bathhouses clean.

The old cafeteria was a Government-type building with an A-shaped roof. On weekends (I wasn't old enough to go), they'd have dances down there and they really did "boogie." Then, Sunday mornings they turned the building into a church, and we'd have services there. When they got ready to close that building down, it was really a heartbreaking thing. It took away all the recreation. They took it down when Oak Ridge was becoming less secretive and more of an open-type city. When they began to build more permanent-type houses, that community was dissolved.

Then I moved with my family to a flattop on a street now known as Houston Avenue. It was more of a family-type building—it had a kitchen, bedroom and bathroom. We stayed there for about a year while they were building the permanent houses in Gamble Valley. And that leads to my street name. Originally, Gamble Valley was an all-white, working-class community. Then it was set up primarily for black people. They named the streets after black universities and colleges.[3] Just in case you looked sort of blonde in Oak Ridge or somebody might mistake you for another race, after you gave your address they would know exactly who you were. Because you would either say, "I live on Spellman or Fisk," or "I live at Dillard, Wilberforce, Benedict, Bethune or Bennett." It was during that time that we moved from Houston Street into a permanent residence, and that's where I live now—in that community, still in Gamble Valley.

Gamble Valley is completely different today. In the beginning, as I said, we had this tepee-like place. Now we've living in a regular house. When we moved into the permanent housing, they were mostly duplex, and then they had some family housing according to what you could afford. We could only afford the duplex type. They had two bedrooms, bathroom, living room and kitchen. We were really "uptown." Beautiful hardwood floors, windows, doors and things. (The Hutments had wooden flaps or shutters, no window panes, only screens. I used to have to let the flaps down and close the shutters.) So we had real window panes that went up and down and a big front yard and a small porch. As far as housing was concerned, the standard in Oak Ridge was quite nice.

In the early days, we had a certain type of people. Most of the black people who came here were laborers etc. They settled and stayed here, and the women did mostly all of the domestic work for the white people in town and kept their houses.

As time went on, you had a turnover. The black women wanted to work in the plants, and so did the white women. So those white women who could afford somebody coming in and cleaning up the house realized that if the black women went to work down at the plant, they would lose their good help. For a while, there was a sort of warring between the two groups. It was so blatant. For instance, you'd see Oliver Springs, Clinton and Knoxville black women working in the plants. Oak Ridge black women were domestic workers. They weren't hired at the plant because it would rob somebody of a good maid. All this came out later. I don't know if this has been written about or anything.

Was I conscious of the fact that Scarboro School was segregated from the white community when I was growing up? Honey, I was conscious of the fact that I was segregated against from the day I was born. I mean, that was a way of life. You were born black, so you just did not expect to do certain things. And believe me, it made me sick. I was quite angry about it. Of course, I am of the so-called black revolution age. I was in that because I was boiling. I was really upset about it. One of the things that used to bother me most was not being able to visit our public libraries.

---

[3]The colleges were named after people, the streets after the colleges.

During that time, we had just gotten over this war. We had bombed out those Japs and Germans and my uncle had come home with half his arm blown off, and friends had been killed in this war with these people. So, the war was over and America was *embracing* these people that were our enemies, but she had her *foot* in my *face*. I felt like that. Because these very people that we had fought could come over here, go to the public library and go anyplace in town—anyplace! There wasn't a place they couldn't go. He could move up here on Stanton Lane, the white section at that time, and it would be perfectly O.K. But there I was. I couldn't go to the public library; and if I was in the ten-cent store and I wanted a Coke, I had to get it and run.

I wasn't even aware that this city had been built by the government on a segregated basis. My view was of the whole country. It wasn't just the city of Oak Ridge. I had been taught in school the Preamble, the Gettysburg Address, and the Pledge of Allegiance, and I loved my country. I felt, and I have written it, that I was a stepchild. I felt worse than Cinderella. I felt like Cinderella, but my prince had never come. I hadn't been rescued yet. I hadn't been found. I was Sleeping Beauty, and my Prince Charming hadn't kissed me and awakened me yet.

Meanwhile, my stepmother and stepfather were about to kill me. I felt real, real bad. So when I was given the opportunity, when somebody said, "Well, look it's time to wake up and do something," I was ready. I was really ready to actually die. Because I thought, "Well, my lord, surely if Uncle Charlie can lose his arm for his country in fighting to keep some other countries across the seas free, surely I can give my life so that my child won't have to have this feeling." It's a terrible feeling.

My grandmother worked for people that I stood in awe of. He was a judge and a man highly respected in the town by all people. Because of this, my grandmother was highly respected. When she walked into a store—I don't care who was there, white, black or who—she was waited on first because she was Judge So-and-So's cook or maid. "She's coming here shopping for him." (This was in La Follette, Tennessee.) So this feeling started before Oak Ridge. My feeling at that time was not against local Oak Ridge government.

Lavada: Before I first came to Oak Ridge, I lived in Knoxville about three or four years. I came from a little town in the middle of Tennessee—Murfreesboro—about thirty miles south of Nashville. In 1944, I heard of Oak Ridge. I had just finished high school and I was looking for a job. I wanted to go to college, and of course, I couldn't go to college. That same year my mother had passed, and I had to get a job.

So I came to Knoxville and got a job. I started to work in Gamble Valley. They had a trailer camp there at that time. I was a maid. We cleaned up the wash houses. (I was very young then—about 18.) One time a group of black ladies and I were working and a lady came in and said, "I'm tired of these wash houses being half-clean!" The girl working with me cursed her out. That frightened the lady—a black girl cursing a white woman! Only white people lived in the Gamble Valley trailer camp. There were trailers all over the hill and all the way back behind the school—nothing but trailers then.

After seven months, I stopped and took Cosmetology in Knoxville at the Lady Alice Beauty College. When I completed that course, I came back to Oak Ridge and worked in a beauty shop down at the Hutments until they got ready to move.

They had all the women in the Hutments penned in. I don't think they had any fence around the men's Hutments. The women were actually fenced in— you couldn't see over it; it was about ten feet high. They had guards at the gates for them to go in and out. I don't remember seeing any passes, but I guess it was a kind of gentlemen's agreement that they knew everybody who could go in or out. It was that kind of thing that they had with the people who lived there. Men were not allowed to go in there, but the women could come out and go to the men's huts. That's the way it was. Some of the women had husbands living in the men's huts, but they could not live together. At first they didn't have any housing for families, and they didn't allow any children on the area—they just didn't have the facilities. But later on they built family huts, it seems as if they had some at the J.A. Jones Construction Co. somewhat before the '50s. That's when things began to change.

Tommy: I remember I had a badge and I lost it. I got in on Aunt Ruth's badge. We used to laugh over that—you know, "They all look alike."

Lavada: And I remember one time that a black man said that he had a monkey's picture and he just stuck it in the frame of his badge. He just flashed it at the guard and came on in.

Where I worked, it was just called the Woodland Area. When they moved the Scarboro School near Gamble Valley, the residents decided to call the section after the school, and it is still called Scarboro. They didn't want to call it Gamble Valley, which was named after a white man who owned the land, and, of course, it's in a valley. Scarboro School was started when black children came to the area, about 1948, when Mrs. Officer became the first principal.

Tommy: The black community had a Chapel on the Hill, but there was a distinct difference between it and the Chapel on the Hill in the white community, which still exists, although the names are the same.

Lavada: Now you take the white people, so to speak. Lots of people came here looking for jobs, just as I did, looking for a better way of life and looking for whatever I was looking for. And they were in a struggle, trying to find work to do. They came from rural areas, and some came from cities. They needed a job, too; they needed work.

Tommy: Oak Ridge was a distinctly different city from Clinton, Oliver Springs and Knoxville. It was like going to another state.

Lavada: The pay was better, but the blacks got paid less for the same kind of work. But even if their pay wasn't as high, it was a job. It was better than not having anything. Because a lot of places, people didn't have jobs. So that was one of the main things. Lots of people—both black and white—hadn't worked. They didn't have anything to do. Just the idea of having a job made their condition better.

Tommy: This is the point I want to make. That Oak Ridge was very, very different from the surrounding towns. Actually, I felt when I would leave Oak Ridge—like going back to La Follette—I was really discriminated against. Because this is the difference I was going to tell [Lavada] Chisholm in the white and blacks. Yes, there were many white people coming here looking for jobs. But Oak Ridge was mainly white-oriented. You had more scientists and more professional people that were on that level. The basic people who came here were engineers and scientists.

These whites used black household help from Oliver Springs and Clinton. These people just worked here and then went back home. But the black people who came into the city to work from Mississippi, Alabama and around, these were black people who stayed. So you had this almost illiterate black people and this very high, intellectual white society that lived in the city of Oak Ridge.

Lavada: You shouldn't say that across the board like that, because there were a lot of white people who hadn't an education, but they were here. It wasn't only the highly technical, professional white people and illiterate blacks. There were lots of illiterate whites here digging ditches etc., and they were in competition with each other.

Tommy and Lavada: Within the framework there, you had this old policy where you would pay a black laborer less than you would pay a white. They'd be doing the identical thing.

Lavada: Some whites would be working on a higher level. But if they were digging ditches, it was the same thing. You know, there's no difference in the way a white man or a black man could dig a ditch. But if they were digging ditches, they would pay the white man more than a black man—maybe $1.50 an hour and the Negro $1.00. I know a lot of them worked for that. I'm sure they did.

Thelma Present: What other ways did you feel that Oak Ridge was different? Let's say, when you went out of the city. What was the contrast?

Tommy: When I went out of the city as a child, I was treated differently by the whites in the same socioeconomic group as the whites in Oak Ridge. The whites in Clinton or La Follette looked down on me and treated me differently. The Oak Ridge students treated me as an equal.

I know we were all here, white and black, struggling, trying to make it. But there was that certain difference, and I could feel it when I left the city of Oak

Ridge. I can remember some of the people who were around and I was around them, and they were just very intellectual people, and they treated me just like I was a person. But they had a different attitude toward the blacks. They had a different language, even.

When I attended high school in Oak Ridge, it was segregated. I think it was integrated the first year I moved from the city —about 1951 or 1952. In the black high school at first we were bused to Knoxville. I was too young then. By the time I was in high school, they had a volunteer high school. You see, the thing about it is this. What Lavada was saying is that the same bloodline that was back before the war and during the war—with the gates closed and then gates opened—it still runs. I mean the strain is still running, and it runs right through the city of Oak Ridge.

[But there were] these people in the city, who I felt were quite liberal at that time, and that's why I felt the pressure when I left the city and met other white people. But these [Oak Ridge] people, even with their liberal attitudes, did not feel that their children should go to school with black kids— some of them. That's why we had the old Scarboro School.

Lots of these white people had feelings. They were concerned, and for that reason some of them felt it was terrible for black children of Oak Ridge to be bused into Knoxville in order to get a high school education. Those liberal people of Oak Ridge thought that. So what they did was organize a school. They called it Scarboro High School. People who were scientists and physicists and things around here in the city volunteered their time and would come over to the school. There were some very famous and outstanding people in the first Scarboro High School. That's why I say I had a real good education. Our first graduation class consisted of three students, and the next year we had three students graduating. I must have been in the eighth or ninth grade when the Scarboro High School started. Anyway, they volunteered their efforts. But still they were keeping us segregated. I don't know whether they wanted to or not. But what they could have done was to say, "O.K., there are three students in the senior class, so many in the freshman, sophomore and junior classes. We'll send you all over to Oak Ridge High School."

Lavada: Wasn't that against the state law for blacks to go to white schools? Then they couldn't put you there because of the law.

Tommy: Maybe that was the reason, I don't know. But I do know that a few years later, they did integrate Oak Ridge High School—whether the state law was there or not. It was one of the first schools in Tennessee to integrate.

Lavada: There were some people who didn't want us in the white schools and they picketed.

Tommy: Even if I hadn't had the advantage of being taught by those volunteer teachers, I wanted to go on with my education, because my grandmother said so. And it rang through my whole life up to today. I appreciate what those teachers did, but she was the main person in my life. She always wanted me to go to school, because she thought it was very important. Even if I had never had the benefit of those teachers, I would have found a way. But every now and then, I run across a paper that had been written by somebody who has touched my life somehow or other as a child over at Scarboro School. It's quite a feeling. I'm a librarian now, and I handle a lot of technical reports, papers, etc., with the Department of Energy Technical and Information Center.

Lavada: I'm an elementary school teacher. I was educated at Knoxville College. I went back to school about ten years ago.

Today in Oak Ridge, I feel that we have more opportunities than we had in the beginning to a degree. I think we're in the stage where we've gotten to the table.

Tommy: We've moved up a little bit—to where Lavada has just got through saying. But we haven't really gotten started.

Bettie Levy, a white woman from Southern California, was one of the many disturbed by Oak Ridge's segregated start. Looking back in an 1980 interview, she talked about how things might have been different and better:

I felt very strongly that it was a disgrace that the city was started on a segregated basis. The Federal Government tried so hard to do things right. They thought that since Oak Ridge was in the South, they did not want to stir up any trouble or call attention to the place. They kind of overdid it. East Tennessee is not the Deep South. They could have gotten away with a much milder policy than they followed. I happened to be the one who was taking someone from the Federal Bureau of Budget around when I was working for the AEC. He needed to review some of the problems about the turnover of money as we changed from the Manhattan District to the AEC. He was absolutely horrified. He said, "You mean the Federal Government has done something like this!"

In the war years, they didn't think through clearly, but then rectified it reasonably well. Some people worked very hard to push desegregation, and we have to be pretty proud of our school system. I think it was the principal and two teachers who went around, gave talks and did a lot of preparatory work toward what we used to call integration. We never achieved that, but at least we eventually got desegregation. The schools worked very hard to try to make that a smoother change.

Letter IV

Dear Margaret,

It gets "curiouser and curiouser."

Last week our publicity group wanted to hold a meeting, and since all of us had children, we decided to meet one afternoon. One girl offered her house with a fenced-in yard complete with sandbox and playpen. We were seven women, eight children (six months to six years) and two cars. A half-hour before, the cars made the rounds picking up mothers, babies, bottles, diapers, pails, shovels and what-nots. It was quite a sight to see us marching in. The kids were dumped in the yard—three babies in the playpen—and we held our meeting. It went surprisingly well, and we all had a good time.

I find that I am alternately depressed or stimulated and amused by the life here.

For a while we had difficulty getting out at night. Twice in succession two high school girls promised to "sit," and neither showed up or even called. The second time I called the girl's home and her mother said she had left an hour ago to stay with a baby. She asked me to have the girl call when she arrived. I must have, unwittingly, "cooked her goose." When I complained to friends, most of them grinned. It seems as if these high school girls have a little racket. They tell their parents they're off to keep babies, and instead keep their dates.

Well, I have two more lined up. One girl's father drives her here and calls for her. Then we have another who is very fat, and, I suppose, not too attractive to the boys. Her mother told me she likes to "sit" and spends all her earnings on candy and ice cream. I have heard of some who have given up the

45

hunt and arrange with neighbors to keep their telephone off the hook. And others have worked out a sound device that can be projected to a neighbor.

I spent an interesting evening with a girl who lived in a section called Gamble Valley for over a year. This is an all-trailer colony, with a conglomeration of laborers, technicians, G.I.s and people from all parts of the country. When they moved there, the Government supplied the trailers to the workers, but there were no provisions for enlisted men (with families).

Her husband was a G.I, and in order to be together with their child, they bought a trailer—as did others. Those who owned theirs took pride in keeping it clean, but most of the others didn't care. The interiors were filthy. The children were dirty and unkempt and ragged. Most of the parents showed little interest in the children, and there were many instances of real meanness. The trailers were almost piled on top of one another. There was no privacy and lots of squabbling which everybody could hear. There was a great deal of loose living, drunkenness and wife exchanging. One man discovered his wife in bed with a soldier and killed him. A lot of the young girls, having been exposed to all this, became prostitutes. There was a tremendous amount of racial prejudice—and all sorts of religious cults and sects. Because of the overheated trailers, dust and mud, there were lots of colds. They even threw salt on the road to overcome dust, and this resulted in rusted and corroded fenders.[1]

Then there was the constant struggle for food. This was general throughout O.R., because, at first, there weren't any stores on the area. Marketing was done in nearby towns with people pooling cars and baby-tending. Also garbage collection was irregular. This was particularly bad for Gamble Valley because of the close quarters, and in the summer the flies and heat were unbearable. There was also a terrific shortage of all foods. The milk was reconditioned, eggs mostly rotten, no fats at all, and hardly any meats or vegetables. Lots of people depended on packages from home—including boiled eggs. Also in the beginning, there was hardly any means of recreation, and in Gamble Valley the teen-agers went wild to the extent of breaking through the wall of a building. Eventually, the Army built them a recreation hall, and tried to clean up the colony. They still haven't been entirely successful. Oh yes, many of the workers were working ten hours a day, seven days a week, and making exorbitant salaries, and spending it quickly.

In spite of all that sordidness, people showed wonderful generosity in times of need. If a mother-in-law was expected to visit, neighbors would help clean the trailers. One woman went to the hospital for her second baby and neighbors cared for her boy and prepared meals for her husband. They even had flowers all around for her homecoming. All this makes wonderful material for stories and I think she is going to write them up.

More data about early O.R.:

Problems of pregnant women: No maternity clothes available; worries

---

[1]Herbert Pomerance, one of those I interviewed, said that so many complained of eye trouble from the dust that the first road to be paved was to the hospital.

about riding on the buses with roads unpaved and full of holes; hospital was still being built, and one of the first pregnant women here had her periodic examinations behind a makeshift screen with a sheet around it while there was hammering around her. It was a race between her baby and a delivery room.

Couples living apart would come and watch their house being built. Most people were wary of each other, and conversation was limited because of all the secrecy. The first question women would ask was where their husbands worked. Husbands would want to read all letters written and would sometimes strike out whole pages. Certain words were "taboo." Very few had phones, and when some men would work overtime, they had no way of contacting their family. There was a great deal of antagonism in the surrounding towns—particularly Knoxville—against these foreigners who dragged mud and red clay wherever they went. Most of the women wore slacks because of the crowded, dirty buses (many a time they had to sit on the floor with their packages), and that also annoyed the Knoxvillians.

Then there are amusing stories about the people who first moved into the new houses. There was a constant stream of plumbers, carpenters, electricians, etc. You never planned on taking a bath between 8:30 and 4:30. Those pass keys must have been a nightmare. A woman would come home from marketing and find a workman drinking beer in her kitchen and listening on the radio while waiting for his pickup car. They would track up the floors with mud and twigs and then put the shellac over it. One couple spent weeks scraping it off with steel wool, the only thing available for the purpose.

We have been trying to get our yard fenced in for weeks. We have changed the gate on our porch to four different places, and Irene has figured out how to escape each time. You need a permit for almost anything you want here, and each request requires a lot of red tape. The Army still has overall control, but contracted with the Roane-Anderson Company to manage the town, houses, hospital, restaurants, stores, telephone, laundry and everything else. They, in turn, had concessionaires run these things. This was all supposed to be at hardly any profit. Anyway, with all this, you can imagine how much satisfaction you can get when you make a complaint. They just wear you down referring you to dozens of people. Most of the time you feel as if you have come against a stone wall, and wait weeks for satisfaction, if you get it at all.

We have had several occurrences. They are starting to permit some private business here. I think bids are submitted. For instance, the maintenance of the homes has been taken over by a company called Tri-State. They still have to answer to the Army. But about three or four enterprises are entirely private.

The reason I haven't written for a few weeks is that I have been getting some medical treatment, and have been going to the hospital several times a week. There are a few doctors[2] now having private practices, but none of

---

[2]During the war, all medical men, including dentists, were from the Army.

them have private offices! So everyone has to go to the hospital for any kind of treatment. Originally, all fees were fixed and there was a good hospitalization plan. Of course, you couldn't choose your doctor and had to wait your turn and it was very clinic-y, but everybody was served. From reports, the obstetrics department was excellent. There, too, you weren't in the hands of any one doctor but whoever was on duty, so you never knew who would deliver your baby. But now, the private doctors who are coming in are permitted to charge whatever they want. But my experience has been that the fees are steep and certainly out of proportion to the average earnings here. My doctor is a Southerner and bitter about socialized medicine. He also claims this is a "socialistic" town. I hope socialism will never be like this.

If the tone of this letter is less cheerful than usual, blame it on the rain. I struggled with the furnace all morning.

I had put our muddy rubbers outside, and when Dick went to get his, they were full of water. Our newsboy tracked up the porch with red clay, and someone called up to tell me some malicious gossip. But someone got me a pound of butter (the first we've had since we came) and sour cream from Knoxville. That saved the day.

And that reminds me, if you come bring rubbers and old shoes.

It seems as if I'll never catch up with the things I want to, but enough for now.

Regards from us all.

[sig] Thelma

The secrecy of Oak Ridge runs through many of my letters and the interviews that followed. It was pervasive, and often harmful to morale, although, in compensation, some liked the safety of a closed city. Gus Robinson, the out-of-uniform Army sergeant who had been brought in by General Groves to be the top man in the Army's public relations setup, told Laffitte Howard, then Associated Press correspondent in Knoxville, that the nearest thing to espionage the Army had found before the bomb was dropped was two instances in which a rumor became widespread. This rumor, Robinson said, was that working in the Oak Ridge plants would make the workers sterile, and both times it cropped up at so many places about the same time that he was sure it was planted. By whom he could only guess.

Yet this secrecy, despite its being as ever-present as the mud and dust, had its funny sides. "Gallows humor" came easily when the fate of the world hung in the balance in Europe and the Far Pacific.

Bettie Levy tells one tale:

My favorite story—not a personal story, but one that everybody heard—is about the man who quit working because he saw them bringing in all these trainloads of material and they never took anything out. He figured it was all going into some hole, and he didn't want to work for any project that was not accomplishing anything. That was a local person.

Ida Coveyou was too busy to be bothered by the secrecy, but she also recalls some amusing stories:

Even with all the secrecy and though I worked for a short time as a junior physicist [at Monsanto], when people talked to me about the work, I didn't always understand the reference because I had a liberal arts background rather than a scientific one. With almost all my friends working at the lab, I had no feeling of secrecy. We didn't go back and forth much, so I was hardly aware of the gates or the showing of passes either.

But we did hear wild stories. There was one about the guy who couldn't find his badge. So he took a dollar bill and folded it so that just the picture of Washington showed on top. And they let him in!

Interestingly, some scientists, who had been working for the Manhattan Project in Chicago earlier, told me that they could not read the reports that they wrote!

Later, somebody I knew told me that he ran a haberdashery in New York City during the war. He received a large order for women's underclothes from a place called Oak Ridge. On the map it was listed as a place of seventy-five people. And he thought, "What are they doing with all these women's underclothes?" But he filled the order. Three weeks later, he got another tremendous order for women's underclothes. And he began to think, "My God, they're running a prostitution center for soldiers or sailors there! Or something like that."

Charmian Cohn accepted the fact that her husband's work was secret—as did most wives—and made no attempt to pry. A few women, she said, implied smugly that they knew what was going on, but there was no evidence that they did. At gatherings, when some men drifted into small groups to talk shop, they spoke in a code that they had developed.

Laffitte Howard, as head of the Associated Press bureau in Knoxville and thus the only wire service reporter within 150 miles of Oak Ridge, was almost daily made aware of the size of Oak Ridge and the win-or-lose-the-war necessity of keeping it and its work under cover.

Here is some of what he had to say of those times:

The real secret of Oak Ridge was not *what?*, but *how?* and for *what?*

All mention of splitting an atom, a favorite but science fictionlike topic for many writers in the late thirties, had vanished from newspapers, magazines, and scientific works available to the public. Knoxville was being inundated with men from universities where atom-splitting experiments had been known to be going on. Then, too, the giant electric transmission towers that marched into the restricted area could not be hidden.

The late Loye W. Miller, then editor of the Knoxville *News-Sentinel,* a Knoxville businessman and I discussed this one night at Miller's house early in 1944. The later the hour, the more certain we became that atoms were being torn asunder. I shortly bet a Tennessee Eastman official with whom I shared a house that I knew what was going on—something the Eastman man had no idea about. Our bet was $1, with our landlord holding the stakes.

Within a week, I had the first of three visits from a military intelligence officer—a former Baltimore policeman—and I told him what I was sure I knew and why, pointing out that any third-rate spy from our British or Russian allies or the hostile Germans or Japanese could, and probably did, know exactly the same things. The visits stopped when, on the third trip, the MI officer was challenged to arrest or go away.

Bettie Levy also was told what was going on, but with her prewar certainty that the atom could not be split, scoffed at tales that turned out to be true. But, again, the question was not *what*? but *how*?

Here are Bettie's stories:

During the year I had gone with Henri, who had been working at Oak Ridge throughout the war, I knew there was this laboratory. On three different occasions, while I was living in Knoxville, people told me what was being done at Oak Ridge. Everybody was guessing what was going on at the Clinton Laboratories.

I was rooming in a boardinghouse, and one of the other boarders was a sister of an Associated Press reporter who worked for the national news service. He told his sister one time when he was home on vacation that they had called in these reporters and told them, "Now for the sake of the war effort and for the sake of patriotism, there are three words you are never to use in any news releases. NEVER USE THEM! If anybody says these words, just ignore them, and go on to other things." Well, he was no fool, naturally. I mean, these reporters are pretty crackerjack. He went to the *Encyclopedia Britannica* and looked up the three words and said from his high school and college—just bare required courses in physics and chemistry—he had figured out what they were doing was splitting the atom to get its energy out! His sister told me, "That's what my brother says, and he is really smart." I said, "Ha, ha! I learned physics, too, and I learned that you cannot split the atom. And that is just a pipe dream like perpetual motion." So that was the end of that. If she told me the three words, I have since forgotten.

Then, on a bus, some high school boys were coming home from school, and they were all talking about their physics lesson. They were saying they had figured it out. They went into great detail, discussed it all and said they knew what was doing at Oak Ridge. I didn't believe them either. "These are just high school kids dreaming—the way their minds go."

And the third guess came from a civil engineer working for TVA. He had some friends out at Clinton Laboratories. He said they never said a word to him, but boy! he kept his eyes and ears open. He had figured out just from little things—he knew what their specialties were—and he knew what some of the things were. He said, "I know what's going on there. They are developing a method so powerful for getting the energy out of the atom that one teaspoon of the stuff would blow a crater a mile wide in Knoxville." I didn't say a thing to him because he was an older man, and I wasn't going to just laugh in his face. I thought to myself again, "What a pipe dream!" And that made three times that I had been told exactly what they were doing. Since I am not a physicist, I would never have put it together. But the secrecy and patriotism of everybody was so marvelous that it never got out. It was a secret that was kept.

Henri said that all of the early scientists came at the same time. Because of security reasons, he thinks, they put all of the top scientists in one dormitory in case they might talk in their sleep.

Everything was so secret that whenever anyone asked him what his work was, his standard response was, "Making Hershey bars." He just made that up out of whole cloth. He never gave anybody any other answer. I never asked him what he was doing. I knew he was doing research in chemistry and, really, that was all I wanted to know. I didn't want him to explain any more chemistry than he had to. It mattered nothing to me.

Julia Moore, a teacher who came from Middle Tennessee to Oak Ridge in 1944, told the panel at the Children's Museum that secrecy extended even to the model school system being set up:

In the workshops, especially the first two or three years, we went through a very strict briefing on security. In fact, it grew to be that I couldn't send home a church bulletin to my mother each week, because they didn't want anything that had any names to leave the area. I quit sending home those newspapers called the Oak Ridge *Journal* that I used to roll up. At that time, we were told not to deal with any numbers.

When my county superintendent came to visit me from Maury County and I drove him around the area, he wanted to know how many teachers we had in school, and I said, "Oh, I don't know." He wanted to know how many children. I could tell him how many I had in my class, but I didn't tell him there were three more second-grade teachers. I never did point out that down at the foot of the hill was another school. He never did find out about Elm Grove. They could see Cedar Hill and Highland View, but they couldn't see Pine Valley. And I never told him how many schools there were.

We were also warned not to talk to people in restrooms, lounges, dormitories, cafeterias and any other place. All that was part of the security—not to talk! Not even to ask their occupations, and to this good day, I cannot ask you what you do. It was just so deeply ingrained in me.

Herbert Pomerance was another who found secrecy running through all facets of Oak Ridge life. He talked about it in 1980:

> There was a record-listening club. That was a strange one, because that way you could meet the scientists who were at Y-12. And they were more worried about saying anything about their work than we were. You could talk about music, but they were almost afraid to say they had come from Berkeley.
>
> One joke for me was that one man had been at Chicago with a fellow who had gone to Los Alamos, and he corresponded with him. And in one letter, he said,
> "Do they censor your letters there?"
> He got no answer to the question. So he asked in a second letter. Again there was no answer. The third time he wrote, he said, "If you don't answer, I'll know they do."
> And two days later a security officer came to ask him, "What do you know about Los Alamos? Who told you?"
> He said he was so flustered, so surprised at being asked the question, he replied, "I forgot to tell him, 'why, Arthur Compton told me.' Because we'd had a meeting with the whole professional staff at X-10 at which Arthur Compton spoke to us about the project."
> So we talked among ourselves, but we found other groups that were unwilling to. A fellow who had married a good family friend and had divorced her went to work at K-25, and I met him several times. But it seems he had a big mouth and they threw him out of Oak Ridge for talking too freely. I was asked about him, I was asked the question, "Did you ever talk of the purpose of the project or the power of what it could do?" And I had to tell the fellow, "No, because we both knew we didn't have to talk about it."

I asked Ruth Carey what her reaction was to the secrecy of Oak Ridge, and she said it was exciting and interesting—that people were glad to do it, to do something positive, because the country was so united in the war effort.

I said, "You couldn't discuss anything with your husband, of course." She replied that she just knew not to do it, pointing out that she wore a badge and had the same security restrictions as her husband, who told her to be very careful. "So you just didn't ask him any questions; you just knew better."

But if secrecy was sacred to the many, Laffitte Howard found a way—in no way connected with his job—to get a better look, by moonlight, at the size and shapes of some of the city's monstrous buildings. His way was as old as those of a man and a maid—he just dated a girl who lived there:

> I met a girl from Kingsport at a Knoxville party who was working for Tennessee Eastman in O.R., and she agreed that I could come pick her up for a movie in Knoxville a couple of nights later. At the gate, my name was on a list and I was checked off and waved through. I noticed that only the time of my

arrival was written down, so when I brought her back, I "got lost" and drove for miles through the area. Of course, all I could see was the outside of enormous buildings, but I was never challenged.

Development of any project the size of Oak Ridge—even one about which there was no secrecy and which was known to be of sure benefit to an area—is bound to bring dislocation of men, materials and mores. So you can imagine how much more was the impact of this top-priority city of secrecy, whose role in saving the Western World was such that it had to grab whoever and whatever it needed with no delaying for feelings-saving negotiations. (When copper wire ran short, silver ingots from Fort Knox went into crucibles and became wire to carry current that would split the atom.)

I was discharged from the Army in November 1943, and came to Knoxville with the Associated Press. To me came queries from all parts of the nation about contacts with a "Manhattan District" for this place called "Oak Ridge," inquiries which died of censorship as I referred them to the War Department in Washington.

Closer home, Knoxville store operators, manufacturers and housewives were growing increasingly restive as almost any worker—from technician to household domestic—was gobbled into the maw of the mystery city.

By the fall of '44, some East Tennesseans were near revolt. Businesses, offices and plants—already depleted by calls to military service—were crippled further by workers leaving for Oak Ridge. Women accustomed to gracious living were finding it not so gracious to cook and clean houses built to be cared for by a staff of servants.

Gus Robinson, himself a Southerner, and perhaps Colonel Nichols relayed the unrest to General Groves and cited the danger of growing refusals to cooperate with the project.

Always a man of action, General Groves invited about one hundred of the area's most influential men—including the editors of the two Knoxville dailies and me—to meet with him. We gathered in Knoxville, were bused to Oak Ridge and driven past the giant plants, while a guide on each bus gave vague figures about the size of the buildings. Next we went to an assembly hall while the General moved among us, chatting like any good host and seeing that highball glasses were kept filled. Then dinner—thick steaks, a rarity for all in those meat-rationed times.

When plates were empty, the General rose. "Gentlemen," he said, "you have seen the size of what we are doing. All I can tell you is that every financial loss, every inconvenience we have caused you, will be worth it. I have to ask you to take my word for that."

He sat down and such was the force of the man's personality that bitter complaints turned into wry, shame-faced grumblings, and things stayed that way until the bomb fell.

Letter V

Oak Ridge, Tenn.
April 26, 1946

Dear Margaret,

Dick had to go to K-25 today, and I went along for the trip. It is about a half-hour ride from here by bus (the only way you can get around here, except by car), and the countryside was beautiful. Of course I was not permitted past the entrance, but from the outside it is an impressive sight. A city within a city and teeming with activity, it is entirely enclosed by a high wire fence and heavily guarded.

One of the things that still strikes me in O.R. is seeing almost everyone wearing their badges prominently displayed all the time. You see them even at social gatherings. For a non-working resident, there is little occasion to wear them unless you want to get a library card, leave the area, and, I suppose, for other incidentals.

It is hard to believe that O.R. is less than three years old. I have just gotten access to the earliest issues of the Oak Ridge Journal, and through it—plus talking to some of the "first settlers"—I have gotten a good picture of the growing pains and development of a new city built according to specifications.

O.R. started June 15, 1943, and the first issue of the Oak Ridge Journal came out September 4, 1943. It was mimeographed, started with eight pages about five by eight inches. Starting with the December issue, there appeared the following under the title: "Published for O.R.—Keep it here."

I couldn't resist copying a message from the town manager because it typifies that period. It would take pages to write a digest of these papers, and if you are interested, I shall get to it some day. But from some of the personal stories, O.R. was quite a different place in the "old days." Most of the people who were eligible to live in so-called permanent homes—and they included all professional people, select Army officers, select personnel and manager groups, all having families—came here before houses were available. One family of three with a fourth on the way doubled up with another family of four in a C or three-bedroom house. In another instance, there were six adults in a B or two-bedroom house. And so it went. They would watch their houses being built. For example, say twenty houses were being built. One day all the foundations would be laid, the next day the walls would go up. Then all the porches, etc. And suddenly, there was your house.

In those days, living was very informal, people shared everything. There was a general air of excitement. Some of the highlights were the openings of the first 5 & 10, the first movie, beauty parlor, the first bus, etc. Then they began to get telephones. Well, in spite of the extreme hardships, these people feel those were the happiest days here.

Apparently as things improved physically, the spiritual unity dispersed. Today, much of the big happy family has broken up into all sorts of feuds. Some of the beginnings were when the first telephones were installed. There was resentment and antagonism towards the first ones, and jealousy. In spite of the inner cliques among the oldtimers—and that was because of the class structure of the husband's position depending not only on what company he was with, but what job he held there—some have become patronizing and indifferent to the newcomers. On the whole we were treated extremely well upon our arrival, but our case is not usual. Most newcomers feel very lonely and muddle around until they reach their level. That seems to be pre-destined.

This all must sound as if I am not happy here. Actually there is a great deal to recommend O.R. There is so much to see and discover, and we are flourishing with the wonderful air and scenery.

Oh, I noticed today that there are two unions here. The United Laundry Workers and the United Chemical Workers. There may be others.

I must tell you of an amusing story of an acquaintance who went off with her husband one weekend and left their little girl with a 16-year-old "sitter." When they got home, their house was almost wrecked. The kid threw a party Saturday night, and there were cigarette burns on the furniture, the Victrola was broken, carpets stained with liquor, and in the bedroom, they found a piece of chewing gum on the side of the bed.

I have heard lots of tales about the prefab dwellers. There is one section where thousands of them are located, and there are many "hill" folks from Kentucky. Naturally, they brought their customs with them. Some of the children start smoking at two years. One father offered his two-year-old a cigarette and she said, "Don't mind if I do." When he offered to light it for her, she said, "kin light m'own." Occasionally you see a prefab stuck in among the "perms." Lots of "perm" dwellers resented this quite audibly, and one woman was heard to admit finally that "the poor things have to live somewhere." Most of the children go barefooted.

Several of the women who have had their babies here have stories. Most of them were very young and inexperienced. All of the babies were breast-fed in the hospital. That was a rule. When they got home, those who wanted to give bottles were all given the same formula. They couldn't depend on much pediatric care, and when the formulas disagreed with the babies, most of them tried various ones they got from baby magazines. The House & Garden Baby Book was a "bible" to many of them. One mother called the hospital because her baby was constipated. The doctor asked her if it was breast-fed, and when she said it was, he said all breast-fed babies got constipated. A few weeks later, the baby developed diarrhea. She got the same doctor and he asked her the same question. His answer was that all breast-fed babies got diarrhea. In many cases, the husbands stayed home from work several days when the wives came home. And that is one thing about O.R. The fathers do pitch in a lot and have great interest in their children.

Well, Margaret, I have been raving on at such length that I wonder sometimes if I bore you. We should love to know how you, Gregory and Cathy are getting along.

Best to all of you.

[sig] Thelma

Ida, who was from Chicago, had some interesting experiences centering around the differences in culture and language. Here is part of her account:

At Monsanto, where I worked, I made the deductions for the bookkeeping department for the housing for all of the people who worked in the Oak Ridge National Laboratory. And since we got our housing from the labs, our rent was taken out of our paycheck.

I remember discussing this with the bookkeeping department. At first there had been a flat fee for the month. Then they decided that each month would be figured on a daily basis. So each month our rent was different—depending on the number of days. I didn't understand why they made this complication, but when they made that change, some people came to see me to kick about their rent change. One time a group of hard hats came into my office, and I stood at the window and talked to them for about fifteen minutes. After they made their initial outcry and their initial gripe, they never said another thing to me, but stood there and smiled. I thought I had told them what they wanted, but after they left, the other girls told me, "Ida, they didn't understand one word you said to them with your Northern accent. They had no idea what you were saying."

But, you know, we did have little run-ins that a lot of us didn't recognize, because there were such differences in the culture. In Chicago, I could say almost anything like, "It rains a lot," and nobody cared. Well, it rains about twice as much here, and I mentioned it to some girls from Knoxville. They really acted quite hurt and insulted, and I couldn't figure out why. All I said was, "It rains a lot." They exploded, "You all come here from big cities and think you can wear any old stuff. You wear dirty and muddy shoes and you don't think it's important, because you think you can do anything you like with us. It doesn't make any difference!"

It never occurred to me, and to most of the other people I knew, that this was a personal matter. Of course, our shoes were muddy. There was nothing but mud around. And who wants to waste all your time cleaning shoes? Most of us had been in college in the '40s, and the popular thing to do in the big Northern schools was to go around with dirty shoes. To come here and start to scrub them was inconceivable. I felt badly about being insensitive to their feelings.

I later moved into the physics division—even though I did not have a degree in physics. My husband was the first male scientist without a bachelor's degree who went on "monthly" at Oak Ridge National Labs, and I was the first woman scientist who went on "monthly" without a degree.

There was another area in Oak Ridge where differences had to be overcome. Newcomers from other parts of the country—particularly from the North and West—had to learn to understand some of the following expressions and different accents:

Poke—not a jab, but a paper bag or "sack" of groceries.
Fir or Fur—not a tree or a pelt. Means "for."
Honey—everybody and anybody was one.
Lack—you either liked it or lacked it.
Precious—an expression of endearment, "He/she/it's precious!" Most often
         used to describe a small child or something one admired.
Yawl or y'all—meaning you or several people. "Y'all come back, hear?"
War—"Let's not fight over the 'wire'."
Wore—"It's not what you think, as it were."

Local people were just as mystified by the talk of many of us "furriners." As an example, a woman newly arrived in Oak Ridge from Chicago told me of going shopping in a supermarket. Along with her groceries, she put a dozen oranges in her "buggy." As she placed the purchases on the checkout counter, the clerk said, "Do you want a poke?" My friend, startled and alarmed, demanded, "What have I done wrong!" The clerk said, "Not a thing, honey. But I'll sack them anyway."

And we had a Mormon woman from East Tennessee who came to "keep" our newborn baby. She offered "raffrinces" and assured me she had no "vahces," 'ceptin' that she "dipped backy." But she "niver" spit the juice in the house. One day I came home and she told me the baby had been bitten by a "warsp," but not to "wurry." She had applied a "ginrus" dab of backy juice—a "ginrul" cure-all—over the bite immediately and the sting was gone from the "pore" little thing.

Kathryn Cantrell also commented on the diversity of those who were to become Oak Ridgers:

> The trickle of workers that started coming into the Oak Ridge area in late 1942 and in early 1943 had grown by the winter of '43 and the spring of '44 to a steady stream; and by the summer of '44, it was a roaring torrent. These people came from everywhere. They brought with them their customs, their mannerisms and accents. But soon after they came, all Oak Ridgers became very adept at speaking a language that was foreign to everybody else in the country. The key word in this language was cemesto. In the cemesto category there were A houses, B houses, C, D and F houses, all with hand-fired coal furnaces.
>
> I came to Oak Ridge in February of '44. My husband had been there since the September before. He was hired by Tennessee Eastman. We were delighted to be together under one roof. I had been home with my folks in Western North Carolina since the birth of our first child.
>
> We were so thrilled to get into that flattop that the first evening that we were all settled we were going to have a celebration dinner. My husband is very fond of biscuits, so we were going to have biscuits. I preheated the oven, I thought; the indicator light came on and I was all set to bake. But when I opened the door, there was not only no heat, there was no oven heating element. In those days, stoves could have only one element because of the metal shortage. Some enterprising soul, who had access to our house before we got there, had taken my oven element. So either he or she could have two elements in their stove.

Rose Feldman, too, looked back with nostalgia at the beginnings of Oak Ridge:

> The early days were fun in a way. First of all, all of us GI wives had our husbands here and not fighting overseas. We knew they were safe. We didn't really know what was going on here, although I had some suspicion because of my background.
>
> Before we left Washington, when Cy went into the Army, I had gone to say good-bye to the people at the Geological Survey with whom he had worked. One of them was talking about the fission work going on in New Mexico. When Cy called me on the phone to say that he was in Knoxville and was going to do some scientific work for the Army—that was all he said—I immediately asked in my usual careless and happy-go-lucky way, "Does it have something to do with fission work?" There was a long silence at the other end of the telephone. I got the hint and shut up. Luckily, nobody was listening.
>
> When I first got to Oak Ridge, I really didn't think of the gates and passes and restrictions. I was just looking forward to seeing my husband. It was just another part of wartime, and we were accustomed to lots of restrictions,

ration books and all kinds of formalities. Our living conditions were different from what we had had in Philadelphia (we weren't exactly prosperous), but I don't recall that I minded any of it. We'd been recently married, and the only home we had together was a rented room. Then we had a small apartment for two years. But compared to what might have happened, it was still pretty good.

We were all young, and we made friends very quickly. Cy arrived on the eve of Rosh Hashona and met several people at the High Holiday services. There were many Jewish GIs, as you can imagine with the large scientific group. The services were held at the Chapel on the Hill, and on that first evening he met Ruth Carey there.

When I came a month later, we went to Ruth's house, which was a little flattop, and there were a dozen GIs there for supper that night in that tiny flattop. Milton, her husband, was on shift work, and we didn't meet him until later. She was sort of a "mother" figure—in her twenties at that time. They all gravitated there. We became good friends with the other GIs and we've kept in touch with some of them.

We lived in the middle room of a C house from the day I came, April 1, 1945, until the GIs were assigned Victory Cottages in January or February 1946 in what is now Gamble Valley—or around Grove Center. Our cottage had much less elegant surroundings than we even had in the C houses—Cy called it our "Pyrrhic" Victory Cottage—but it was our very own.

These cottages, which were a step below the flattops, also had a flattop. They were 28 feet square, up on stilts, and were divided into two apartments, each 14 by 28 feet. None of them had any plantings or trees. They were absolutely bare. There wasn't a tree or a blade of grass in sight. They had a kerosene tank on the outside, which was used for the single, two-burner stove, which had been converted from an old-fashioned wood stove, with an iron top with manhole covers. It was simultaneously a cookstove and a water heater. The bathroom had a toilet, a sink and a little shower. The other room had an old-fashioned sink up on legs and an icebox for which we had a block of ice delivered once a day. We cooked on this furnace unit. The cottage was furnished by the Army with an ancient sofa bed, a linoleum-topped cafeteria table and two chairs.

Cy said it was "surplus from the Civil War."

In the bedroom we had a three-quarter iron bedstead, and that was it! There was no door between the two rooms. We had a crib and a high chair that we fitted in somewhere. We bought an Army trunk, which I covered with cretonne, that we used for our coffee table. We used orange crates for end-tables and for bookshelves. I sewed a strip of cloth onto an Army blanket, which we used for a door between the two rooms so that we could shut out the sounds a little bit in the evening.

We had a seder in that place, guests for dinner and many visitors. We lived there four months. It took almost all day to heat enough water for the laundry, and it got unbearably hot in that tiny space. One April day, when I was pregnant with my second child, I took Joannie out visiting for several hours, leaving the furnace to accumulate sufficient hot water. I wasn't feeling too great, and when we got home the apartment was 117 degrees. A candle bunny rabbit, given us by a friend, was lying in a pool of wax. I did the laundry (on a washing board), including sheets, diapers, uniforms—everything. Then I put on my boots and waded through the red clay. I had a long clothesline and hung all the clothes up. As I put the last one up, the line broke. Everything fell down over me. When Cy came home from the lab, he found me sitting in the middle of the line of wash in the red clay mud—crying!

In June of that year, we were assigned a flattop in the west end of town. We really moved uptown. Those have all been torn down now except some on Outer Drive.[1] The flattop was practically a palace. It was 24 feet square—some 500 square feet. We had an electric stove, a double sink in the kitchen and a pantry. We had a Warm Morning heater, a nice big window to look out of at the woods in the back and a little boardwalk. It was lovely. We had nice neighbors—a shift worker at Y-12 and his lovely wife, who was a school teacher, and two daughters. We had a GI couple across the street, and a really weird, elderly couple next door. Henry was born that October.

New York City
June 5, 1946

Dear Thelma,

You do write such interesting letters and and all the clippings and local color all help to give me a picture of your new life. One of the things I keep wondering about is whether people get sick—especially mentally sick—oftener or less often behind the wires. And you talk of the help the Red Cross gives people, I wonder if they have published any reports of the amount of help they have been? It seems that a while ago an Army officer made a public speech somewhere—I haven't heard exactly where—and pointed to Oak Ridge as the model and perfect community, and this remark was picked up quite a little by the planners. May be important.

Ellwood is pretty out of date. Do they have Myrdol's "American Dilemma" there, that's very interesting. Did you want me to send you "Yankee City"? We're leaving for the country the 16th, and I'll send you a new address before then. This Sunday we plan to spend with a nice English boy whose army team of people are now going to carry on in peacetime and they are so interested in everything happening over here and the way people feel about things like the bomb.

Gregory joins me in sending our best to all of you.

Yours,
[sig] Margaret

Lydia Bredig, a psychologist educated at Cornell and Columbia Universities, came from New York to Oak Ridge, where after a year she set up

---

[1]Hundreds were moved to the University of Tennessee campus to house married students because there was such a shortage of housing in Knoxville.

counseling programs in the Oak Ridge schools and at Oak Ridge National Laboratory. She was also in private practice and in this, particularly, she saw and studied the roles and problems of women in this unique city. In an interview, she told of her slow absorption into the community:

The first year I was commuting from Oak Ridge to New York, still working as a psychological consultant to 2 private schools in New York and really did not settle into the community here. I used that year to find out slowly what it was all about—getting to know the community. I got to know a lot of people. One of them was Dr. Jean Felton, then Researcher of the Medical Division at ORNL. We worked with adults on a voluntary basis, I did some work for the schools, and was invited to give a talk here and there.

The wives were considered to be volunteers, which was the way things were done. It was not until the next year that I became recognized as a professional. I was engaged as consultant to the schools and also started a clinical program at the Laboratory spending half time at each place.

I was the only psychologist when I first came here and was very much overworked. But it was an exploration—completely new. For example, I started out with workshops with teachers, then groups of teachers, rather than working with a single child. I was consultant for problem areas and for ways by which teachers could understand and improve themselves a little better.

I worked with individual women at the Laboratory as the clinical psychologist. My private practice did not expand until '47 or '48, simply because of lack of time. Also, I could not see anyone privately if they were from the lab.

There were a lot of differences in the problems of men and women. The differences depended on why they came here, what their motivation was, how old they were, and at what stage they were. Those women who came here to follow their husbands went through a rather different kind of experience. Other women came and got married here. Some came to leave home; and, wherever they came from, a lot of it was a cultural and economic changover. If you recall, it was coming out of the Depression in the '40s into affluence and job security. So some of the younger women were still having dreams of what they were going to accomplish, and some of them who came here in the early days, before '45, discovered they were much more abandoned.

The wives' intimacy with their husbands had limits. Not so much because the husbands couldn't talk about their work, but because their libido was involved in their work. They expected their wives to make life easier for them. And here, again, the scientists became elite. They had a purpose. A large proportion of the scientists who felt they were elite were psychologically sound. But those who came here with a lot of personal frustration and insecurity couldn't handle it. They expected their wives to take over and support them emotionally. But they couldn't support their wives emotionally. So that a lot of women—and I think these were not only the wives of scientists, but it was true of some wives whose husbands were below the scientific level in the sense of doing supporting work, construction work and technical help—were supposed to carry on. They were supposed to make do and not make demands. So a number of the women formed intense emotional relationships with other women, and the men tagged along; but the men were not as primary in that as they might have been in other situations. So we had a reversal.

The women formed an emotional intimacy which became the focus of a social group. And the men's social group was with themselves and separate. But they went along with their wives.

At first, some of the women went through a lot of anxiety. They were displaced. They did not have the closeness with their husbands that they really wanted; there were walls between these husbands and wives. While they were physically close, they became emotionally separated. That fragility increased, and many developed neuroses.

Part II
Growing Pains

Letter VI

Oak Ridge, Tenn.
May 3, 1946

Dear Margaret,

It was nice to hear from you, although the news wasn't so good. Can you hear me now? I was once quite deaf for a month, so I appreciate your experience.

I shall try to answer your questions as I get more authentic information. Apparently the Youth Group is making remarkable strides. I attended a meeting at which one of their delegates reported on a trip they had made to Philadelphia. One of the newspapers there invited about six of them on an all-expense trip to make informal visits to various schools with their message. They were accompanied by one of the teachers here. In preparation for their journey, they spent a week consulting scientists, not to pose as authorities on atomic energy, but just to have facts clear. I understand there are several teachers who are enthusiastic about their work, and are encouraging and guiding them. If you don't get the copies you want, let me know. They, of course, got excellent publicity and feel that the trip was highly successful.

The enclosed article on domestic help in Knoxville amused me. Apparently the housewives won't admit the real reason. It is not at all difficult to get help here. The average wage is 58 cents per hour, and there are several who commute to Oak Ridge every day from Knoxville. It looks as if they mean to hold onto their higher wages—even if they do have to travel three hours a day for them. Those d——d Yankees! At one time the domestics were intimidated here by the KKK. Some of them still bring their own lunch—they are afraid of being discovered eating with a white person. Of course, there are many who live on the area who are just interested in making enough money to pay for their rent and food. Even though there is a small Negro population here, there have been many problems. It occurs to me that for blacks who lived in Oak Ridge and were exposed to outsiders and their ways, the effects will be widespread and will be worth following up. I begin to see why they prefer to stay on here in those wretched hovels—rather than go "home."

No doubt you have read that Wigner[1] is here now as Director of Research at the Clinton Labs. Don't tell anyone, but Dick saw him the other day having great difficulty getting past the gate. Dick had to run for the bus, but five minutes later he [Wigner] was still having trouble.

"Yankee City" is not in this library. Dick bought "Middletown" for me as a gift, and I took "Plainville" out. I am getting a lot from them. Plainville can't be far from here and is, therefore, of particular interest. Have you read "Kabloona"? It was fascinating to me and has stimulated my interest in Eskimo life.

We went to see "The Bells of St. Mary" last week, and I had a good cry. I was embarrassed to meet some colleagues of Dick's on the way out with my red eyes. I was relieved to find that I was not alone. One of the girls made a curious remark: "Oak Ridge is the sort of place that makes people want to have a good cry." She was from California, and her friend from Chicago.

Remember how I wrote you that I had joined an organization here? Well, part of the publicity committee has splintered off to a writers' group. For some reason, I find that I am part of it. I guess it was inevitable that a book be written about Oak Ridge. We have had several discussions as to the manner it is to be written. We considered a serious, sociological study for one, and since we are amateurs and beginners, we thought of getting an experienced social scientist to write and direct the project, while we gathered the material.

The second idea is to have it on an unpretentious level in keeping with our ability, and through human-interest stories and folklore get our point across. We should also like a prominent person to sponsor us. Then someone said there is no reason why we couldn't work on both ideas. So contacts are being made. I thought, before saying anything about you, I would find out if you are interested in either or both ideas. The practical interest is to raise money to further political activity and to give them publicity. I would be glad to hear your reactions.

Dick is struggling with a vegetable garden, but not hopefully. The soil is almost completely eroded, full of rocks and red clay. But, in order to encourage gardening, they are providing topsoil free to anyone. Lots of people are putting a lot of work in their gardens, and stuff is growing. Anyway, I hope we get better results than from the N.Y.U. campus. As for me, I feel like a full-fledged farmer's wife after using the Sears-Roebuck catalogue for the first time. It is the most carefully guarded and most frequently borrowed book here.

About a week ago, a truck stopped in front of the house and a crew of men got out with planks of wood and a ladder. Without saying a word to me, they began to work. Actually, all they did was lay out the planks and set up the ladder. Then it was 4:30 and quitting time. Upon questioning, I learned that we were being prepared and repaired for a paint job. (All of Oak Ridge is to be painted.)

---

[1]Dr. Eugene Wigner.

A few days later, we were abruptly awakened one morning by violent hammering outside which lasted about a half-hour. Then it stopped and we heard the next house being hammered. The next morning we were having breakfast and a head poked up at our window. There was still another crew out there doing some chiseling. They all politely said "Hi!" and went on working. One of them waved to Irene. And that's the way things are done here. I suppose some day I'll come home and find the house painted inside and out. Won't that be a surprise? We have a choice of seven colors. And there are samples in the post office. The procedure is to go there, pick out your choice, fill out an application designating the color for each room and send it to the East Coast Engineering Co. (Whenever you sign anything or fill out anything, there are at least four copies. Once that is sent, the colors can't be changed.)

We are putting up a fence for Irene, and Dick wants to paint it bright orange, but I doubt if we'll get away with it. We are getting the fence from someone who is "terminating."

In a way this standardization simplifies things. Just think of all the decisions one doesn't have to make. Actually, we don't want our house painted, but we're afraid to say so.

Just to give you an idea of a fraction of the activities in Oak Ridge, I am enclosing a page from the Knoxville paper. There is a little item about the Kentucky Club. There are similar clubs from many other states—Minnesota, N.Y., etc. To be eligible, one must have been born in the state or lived there at some time, visited, attended a college, etc.

Dick was glad to hear about Gregory. He has barely enough time to read the papers these days, but means to write him at the first opportunity. He sends regards to both of you.

Me, too,
[sig] Thelma

In 1980, while I was assembling material for this book, I wrote down some additional recollections about Oak Ridge life:

Imagine someone driving up to your house with a truckful of handmade picket fence parts! Only in Oak Ridge would anyone think of advertising for one. Thanks again to the "swap" column, we got ours, complete, for $15. All we had to do was to dig four post-holes, fit the assembled parts into the posts, and voilà, a fence!

In order to be a true Oak Ridger, you had to have a pet, preferably a dog. I didn't know one breed from another, but a neighbor's adorable (precious!) Chihuahua took my fancy, and we considered advertising for one. In the meantime, we visited a friend whose English setter had just had pups. They were adorable, too. Their mother was skulking somewhere and we never saw her.

In answer to my ad: "Wanted, English setter or Chihuahua. Call . . . ," we got a reply from a woman who had some puppies for sale. Something called Chesapeake retrievers. Those pups were irresistible—again we didn't see the mother around. We wrapped one tiny one in a sweater and brought him home. He fared well and grew and grew and **GREW.** That's how we learned that puppies develop into all sizes. Ours was a far cry from a Chihuahua, and this is truly a tall tale.

Due to the regulations for clearance for all residents and the security of the gates, there was hardly any stealing in Oak Ridge. But our neighborhood had a thief!

The culprit turned out to be our by now huge Chesapeake retriever—named Thurber. We loved Thurber, and oh, how he loved us! He would rise up on his hind legs, throw his paws around any available neck and swish his two-foot, feathery tail, toppling anything within its radius.

But he was full of mischief. A born retriever, he had a favorite sport in which he indulged only after a heavy rain. Because of the resulting viscous red mud, people removed their shoes and left them on their porches before entering their houses. After dark, Thurber would make his rounds. In the morning, we would discover a sizable pile of muddy shoes on our front porch. We would then have to sort them in pairs for the neighbors, who soon knew where to come to reclaim them. Sometimes he went far afield and gathered a larger assortment—not always in pairs—plus any toys (he loved dolls) he might find left out in yards. How many times were we forced to place ads in the Oak Ridge *Journal* announcing what was available! On the whole, though, the neighbors were tolerant and even amused. At first, there were almost as many dogs as children in the city.

The cemesto houses were sturdy—but not altogether. Our house had a field in back. A boardwalk ran the length of it, and at the other end was a convenient shopping center. One day, I set out to market with my little daughter. Our dog insistently tried to tag along. I shouted several times, to no avail, "Go home, Thurber!" Finally in exasperation, I dragged him back and leashed him to the back steps. Halfway across the field, we suddenly heard a thunderous clanging. Then Thurber appeared bounding toward us triumphantly—dragging three porch steps at the end of his chain.

Glancing out the window another day, I saw him loping down the street with what appeared to be a head with long, blond hair, dangling from his mouth. A woman, who had washed her wig and put it in the sun to dry, was lunging after him wailing and pleading, "Thurber, my wig! You've stolen my wig! Please!" It finally landed on our porch, where she retrieved it.

But, alas, his days were numbered. The day two Army police knocked on our door, holding Thurber by his collar, was the last straw. "Is this your dog?"

"Er, yes."

Then they handed me a list of missing articles, a price attached to each one, plus complaints. Apparently Thurber had taken to depositing his stolen articles on random porches, and people were left with either the right or left shoe or none at all. They were not amused at Thurber's fey acts. The miscreant must have known then that this final fling was his swan song. We found a new home for him on a farm—a considerable distance from Oak Ridge where, we hoped, his thieving days would be ended.

Bettie Levy, too, had her share of the paint-at-any-price men:

> Remember the famous crews of maintenance workers? Well, I was out on New Year's Eve at an all-night party. When I got back at dawn, I found a crew of painters doing my dormitory room. They painted all New Year's Day. After that it was a little bit neater, and I got some curtains to make the place livable.

As I had written Margaret Mead, segregation affected the working blacks and was not just a ban on association. Herbert Pomerance also felt this discrimination and tells of its effect on jobs Negroes were allowed to do:

> The laundry, by the way, was segregated because blacks couldn't work in clerical or craft occupations. There was a [black] girl with a college degree. She mentioned that she could read and write, so they let her be the desk woman at the laundry instead of washing at the tubs.
>
> (I then asked him how he felt about the government starting Oak Ridge out on a segregated basis. T. P.)
>
> It wasn't all that much different from other areas either. I grew up in Chicago where there was a small, middle-class Negro community that itself would have nothing to do with the other blacks.
>
> We knew the Army wasn't going to have any trouble. They weren't going to create any controversy. Unfortunately, that became the policy, so it was hard to change it after the war. But we had even a separate gate for the blacks to check in. They also had separate time clocks. In the chemistry lab, everybody had to wear lab-issue clothing. It was laundered at the lab; our work clothes were laundered by the employer. The secretaries, who were white, didn't want to be confused with the black bottle washers and laborers, so each group had a different colored smock, which was lab-issue. Even the soldiers who came there changed from their Army clothes to lab-issue clothes.

I asked Ruth Carey if she, being born a Southerner, was bothered by the government having built Oak Ridge as a segregated city.

She said that it didn't bother anybody at that time, because it was just the way everything was, that she had always had a bad feeling about segregation, but that she had not felt any differently about it in Oak Ridge.

I asked her if living conditions for the blacks were not pretty bad and she replied that "they lived under bad conditions everywhere." She added that the blacks who came here, with very few exceptions, were people who came from the very poor places in Georgia and Mississippi, and that most of them didn't feel that Oak Ridge was so horrible because they didn't know anything much better.

Mrs. Carey said that she knew none of the educated blacks when she first came to the city, but met some later, and that their living conditions were better, though they were still segregated.

But as social mores of the country changed, they changed in Oak Ridge, too, she said, and people became more aware of racial injustices. She recalled that Charmian Cohn told her that Waldo Cohn was almost recalled from Town Council because he was in favor of integrating Oak Ridge schools before the U.S. Supreme Court made it the law of the land. She remembered campaigning for Waldo, whose position was in danger because he "jumped the gun" in advocating integration, but that he had won.

Mrs. Carey said that her daughter, who was in junior high at the time, and a lot of the children of their friends were very excited when the schools were integrated and wanted to do everything they could to make the black children feel at home.

"She and the other kids leaned over backward, and I felt there was a little overkill—that they shouldn't do this because it was an unnatural kind of thing—that they should be more natural . . . . The black kids were in a very peculiar situation—they all were. So in order to do it right, maybe they tried a little too hard. But it worked out fine."

Letter VII

Dear Margaret,

Dick was reading the paper and must have come across an ad by Long-champs, "Why not give MOTHER a real treat on Her day? She deserves nothing less than our Sizzling Platter after slinging you hash all year round," because he suddenly said, "No slaving over a hot stove today, let's go out to dinner." Of course he didn't fool me a bit, but it was fun.

We went to Ridge Hall at Townsite, it is a combination restaurant and recreation hall. It is furnished attractively with several "lounges." The East Lounge usually has open house—for adults. We wandered in there. It is a large room holding about thirty bridge tables. A bridge foursome might be arranged in advance or made up of strangers coming in ones or twos. They usually have a few couples, and about 75 percent are men. Two-thirds of those were in uniform. There is usually someone playing the piano and several people hang around the player, lean on the piano and watch or sing.

The West Lounge is for teen-agers, where they dance to a jukebox or play games. Then there is a long porch with four ping-pong tables—also well patronized. A few times a week the East Lounge is rented out for meetings or club affairs at rather high rates. The atmosphere is "nice" and on the "swank" side.

It has occurred to me recently that all the little children are growing up with no "kin." They don't know what a cousin, aunt, uncle or grandparent is—except for brief visits in a few instances. Further, they have hardly any contact with any old people. I have been wondering if this would have any serious consequences, good or bad. [Emphasis added later. T.P.]

Our colored girl, who is quite intelligent, commutes here from Knoxville

73

every day. Special buses have been running here all along for people coming into the area. The regular fare is 52 cents each way, and these people pay $1.50 a week. This is to be discontinued soon and many domestics are considering moving here. But living conditions are not enticing to many Negroes. According to Matty, a hutment is shared by four people, and it is not unusual for someone to decide to leave the area some day, and pack up all of his and everyone else's belongings in the hutment. There are no facilities in the hutments, except primitive burners, and most of them eat in the cafeteria. Rent is $1.40 a week per person. Living is very "loose."

The colored cottage community, on the other hand, is entirely different. But only families are eligible. A single person is sometimes able to get a room with a family, and can live decently. Most of the domestics prefer to work for Northerners. The Southern women, as a whole, try to take all sorts of advantages with them. As Matty says, "Their sweet ways don't fool you none." There is going to be even more of a problem with housing, etc., shortly. One of the big construction companies is planning to hire about 1,000 more Negroes.

We had a disappointment this week. We had ordered a car way back in January (a Kaiser), and the dealer in Knoxville collected our deposit of $100 two months ago. Dick stopped in to make inquiries, and found out that our chances are slim for a long, long time. Preference is being given to prospective buyers with cars for exchange. This is some kind of a racket they have. Anyway, we found out that Knoxvillians have treated the Oak Ridgers scandalously. Right from the beginning, when they smelt money and a market for almost anything, prices zoomed. The story is that they could always tell an Oak Ridger by the red mud. Not only were all the prices excessive, but they treated them like "mud." They even denounced the Oak Ridgers in their press.

Well, they have gotten smart here. Whenever any of the housewives have to go to Knoxville to shop, they are cautioned to dig out their best clothes, wear hats and gloves and see that their shoes are shined. Since the bomb, Knoxville has adopted Oak Ridge, and is "wooing" it. During the war, there were all sorts of rumors here about spies in Knoxville, and word got around quietly for people to keep their mouths shut there. There is one story of a man who was picked up in a beer joint and plied with drinks and questioned. He claimed that they hadn't gotten him drunk enough to answer their questions, and because he refused, they burned his feet and pulled his toenails off. He reported this to security officers the next day to serve as a warning to others. Parents cautioned children or visitors coming to Oak Ridge not to breathe a word of their destination—fearing consequences.

A young worker went "berserk" the other day. Claimed he had the secret of the A-bomb and was afraid of revealing it to the wrong people. Also, heard about many cases during the war. Apparently it was the secrecy that got many of them. A young mother was in the psychiatric clinic—had rejected her child and refused to see him. A young soldier with a medical discharge was overcome by it and broke down. A young girl tried to commit suicide. (Of course, many of these had past records of some forms of maladjustment, but I understand the psychiatric clinic was always busy.)

New stores and new businesses are opening up every day. The first night-club has been announced with "imported" entertainment, complete with a Palm Room, Main Ballroom, and North Wing. There is a new record shop, which has been eagerly awaited, and a snack bar. The baseball season has started and a car goes around the streets with a loudspeaker urging people to attend. (This car has a long history in Oak Ridge and has served as a sort of "Town Crier.") Oak Ridge is now going "big time," which just adds to the contradictions of the city. We can boast that the mayor lives on our street!

But the most exciting thing that is growing here—outside of our lettuce and radishes—is the YCAC (Youth Council on the Atomic Crisis). The enclosed clippings should give you a good idea of what is happinging.

I hope this letter finds you all cured and the family in good health. Our best to all.

[sig] Thelma

Recreation was much on many minds in Oak Ridge in the prewar and postwar days, and it was an effort to meet this need that brought Helen Jernigen to the city that was to become her home and of which she was to become so much a part.

Here's what she had to say in 1980:

I first came to Oak Ridge in 1944, and my first job was at a place called Happy Valley. Happy Valley was located at the future site of K-25; it was the J. A. Jones Construction Company construction camp. Thousands and thousands of workers lived there in trailers and hutments. It was like a little town: it had a movie theater, cafeterias, a department store, a post office, a bowling alley, and a recreation hall.

It was a very lively place. There were no nights there. There were bright spotlights and loudspeakers on high poles. The music played all night, the lights illuminated everything all night, and there was activity all night. The cafeterias never closed. It was an adventuresome place, a boom town, with all kinds of people. For instance, many American Indians had been brought from Oklahoma to work on the construction of the huge plant. The young Indians were always going around teasing the girls, threatening to scalp palefaces, and war whooping. They put on a great act.

Recreation was uppermost in the lives of a great many of us at that time, being young and single. There was an association called the Recreation and Welfare Association formed in 1943 to provide for a town of 5,000, later expanded to provide, first, for 13,000, then, for 42,000, and finally, for 66,000 people. It was run by a council, which I believe was a sort of board of directors. Recreation was a very big thing.

It seemed there was public dancing every night. I thought that might have

,erated in my memory, but I looked it up in an *Oak Ridge Journal,*
enough, in the course of week, there were fourteen public dances.
included dances in the recreation halls, folk dancing at Elm Grove,
,iwood, and Cedar Hill schools, some square dancing, and dancing in the
carboro community in Gamble Valley.

There were all kinds of things for young people. There were moonlight cruises on the "Lake Queen" over at Concord and picnics at Big Ridge Park with buses that left every Sunday morning. You woke up knowing you could get a bus to Big Ridge, stay all day and come back. There were picnics behind the Chapel on the Hill—a large picnic area where we used to sing around a campfire.

There were nightclubs: one was called The Grove, where meals were served until 9 P.M., and then there was dancing until 1:00 every night. They had trios out of Miami Beach and spent big money. The tennis court dances were literally every night and twice on Sunday. The season opened in early May: Wednesday night you danced on the Jefferson court, Tuesday and Friday at the Jackson Square court, and Saturday was for club nights. Sunday was open house at the recreation halls, so you could dance there, too. From the *Oak Ridge Journal,* there is this quotation in a story announcing the opening of the tennis court dance season: "The concrete floors of the tennis courts have proved no obstacle to jitterbugs in the past. However, prospective rug-cutters are advised to bring their own rugs."

There were bands—somebody named Jim Scott and Buzz Everett, who played a lot. Name bands were brought in by the Carbide Girl's Club—Ted Weems, Jimmy Dorsey and Bobby Burns. Most of the music was recorded by Bill Pollack with an excellent sound system. (Bill is still doing it; he is great, and his sound system is good. We've danced to it for years.)

There were always some dark folk rumors about murders at the tennis court dances. I don't know if this ever happened, but there was always some intimation that dramatic things happened there that we didn't know about.

Nor did time hang heavy for Ellie Pomerance, though she was a "mature" 30 when she came to Oak Ridge. Here's her account of dating and dorms in those early days:

I came on June 6 of 1945. They were canvassing at the Berkeley Radiation Lab, where I was working in the engineering end, and I had gone from designing and detailing to the actual working of experiments. The Radiation Lab also was secret, and I wasn't to contact my family or friends in Berkeley that I happened to know. Originally it had been my hometown, but I had been elsewhere and come back.

I was working at the Naval Air Station in Alameda [Calif.], and someone contacted me there because they knew the kind of work I could do, my background as a three-dimensional artist and in mechanical drawing. You can't say I had any definite title.

In the early part of '45, the Tennessee Eastmen men were coming out and trying to get people from our lab to come to Oak Ridge for the Y-12 [Eastman] Lab. There were 30,000 people working there; so they conned me into going to Dogpatch. Frank Oppenheimer was my boss for over nine months before I left, and I knew a few other men who used to commute back and forth. I knew our project was pretty well established and I might take advantage of seeing Dogpatch. It was too interesting to pass up.

I was in the dorm until the last three months before I got married to Herb. I was in the Guest House, also, until they gave me a dorm room down near Jackson Square. I was not in the category of a secretary or typist; even the salary was different. So I was able to get into a dorm room, but it was a single room with two girls. The other girl worked rotating shifts and I was a day person and slept on a cot. For the first nine months it was that way, and I wasn't in very often.

I was older than most of the girls in the dorm, and I got acquainted by baby-sitting and being invited out. I spent half of my life with a group including the Weinbergs[1] from the first part of June until the bomb was dropped. Then I was going to go home.

For dates, we walked to a movie together from the cafeteria. Then afterwards you always went back to the cafeteria, because that was the only place you could go. The little parlors in the dormitories were so tiny, they could only hold about six or seven people at the same time. I couldn't stand dorm living; it was a little bit difficult. We also went on an overnight hike with the Hiking Club.

But it was still six days a week, although shortly after the war, the work went to five days a week. It was less than a week that I went from Y-12 to X-10 because everybody said, "Don't go away, Ellie, stick around." And I had already gotten into the Little Theater and helped immediately on that and also into music through the Cohns. Since he was from Berkeley, too, of course I helped with the orchestra.

Herbert Pomerance interrupted his wife's interview here to say: "Kay Way had a car and we'd go to Norris. We'd just grab some groceries after work and have a picnic. This was a way of getting together in a larger group." Ellie interjected here that the car was "mighty crowded," and Herbert continued:

When the project at Chicago was cut almost in half in early '45, quite a few people came here, like Alvin Weinberg, Kay Way, Gale Young, and Robert Livingston. The ones who were married could get houses, but the ones who were single couldn't. And they said, "Nuts to you. If you want us to go down there, we won't live in a dormitory." And so the Army said, "OK, we'll make a new rule. If you're over 35 and at a professional level, you can get an apartment." The rule was made for 35 because they knew there would only be about a half dozen.

---

[1]Dr. and Mrs. Alvin Weinberg. He later became director of Oak Ridge National Laboratory.

Letter VIII

Oak Ridge, Tenn.
May 21, 1946

Dear Margaret,

This is "grandmother time" in Oak Ridge, and we are in season. Mother was driving with some cousins and we expected them Friday or Saturday. I went down to get the passes for them on Thursday—just in case. Sure enough, they arrived in Knoxville early Thursday evening and called right after Dick left for a meeting with the passes in his pocket. My first impulse, of course, was to tell them to come right out here, but then I remembered that they couldn't get past the gate without the passes. Fortunately, I was able to track down Dick, and he got someone to drive him to the gate with the passes after the meeting. In the meantime Mother called again, and I was able to tell her to start out from Knoxville and that they would be able to get in. It is quite a business! It is also important to instruct visitors what gate to come in (there are about seven here) so that you can meet them or leave the passes there.

It is easy enough to get guest passes in unlimited quantities. You designate the length of time they wish to stay. The limit is for two weeks, and if your visitor wishes to stay longer, the pass can be extended for another two-week period, etc. The nuisance is getting the passes to your guest, especially if you haven't a car. If you have enough notice, you can mail them. Otherwise, you can kill more hours getting them to the gate by bus. Since Mother has friends and relatives around these parts, I keep busy arranging for them to come here. Barbed wire does a prison make!

I have had many interesting experiences lately. Our group is circulating a petition with reference to rerationing essential food in order to alleviate the suffering in Europe. I took mine over to East Village, which is one of the prefab sections. For several miles you can see nothing but these square

79

houses on stilts almost piled on top of each other. Here you find housed the swing-shifters, guards and laboring classes. Many of the women (some with children) work on the swing shift. I don't know how they manage the care of the children. A lot of them come from the hills of Kentucky, Tennessee, Alabama and Texas. The houses are furnished almost identically with cheap, catalogue furniture. Some are very clean and neat, and others quite smelly.

It took me two hours to cover fourteen houses. I had one refusal from a woman who didn't want to be bothered. But they were all extremely cordial and friendly. Without asking my mission, they invited me in and some dusted off their best chairs with their aprons.

I had to read the petition to some of them—didn't have their glasses—and most of them said, "Caint hurt none, sure I'll sign." I was treated like a visitor and found them eager to talk and be friendly. The last one who signed said she thought I was "the law" at first when she saw the petition. Several of her neighbors were complaining about one of the families on the block. They were from Texas, and she said to me, "you go on in there. I want fer you to see fer yerself." Apparently the parents are drunkards and the mother a whore. When she has visitors, she sends the kids out and locks the door. Then the neighbors will hear one of them yell to the others, "We kin go in now. They're through, the door's unlocked." According to my informant, "They ain't washed but ten diapers in a week. Hit's awful. When I see them dirty old kids, I have me a good cry." Well, I went in and it was a good thing the mother didn't invite me to sit down. The stench was overwhelming and the scene so filthy and disorderly that it defies description. I can't understand how those children looked so gol durned healthy, though. As I was leaving the house (incidentally she didn't sign) the father came running drunkenly down the street looking worried.

My friend from the Kentucky mountains said he must have mistaken me for the F.B.I. That's what they call the Criminal Board of Investigation. Incidentally, the reason the woman from Texas didn't want to "call the law" was because she didn't want to "sign no papers and get messed up with anything."

Today I took the petition around in my neighborhood. Up until now, the only friendliness I have had on this street was with my next-door neighbor, so I was a little hesitant. To my surprise, I was greeted even more cordially than in East Village. It took me two hours to cover eight houses. Practically all of them apologized for not coming over to see me sooner, and I wound up with one woman offering to "keep" for Irene any time; another gave me some good leads as to going about getting a used car; another offered to drive me anywhere on the days she had her car; and they all signed the petition.

I have heard from many people here that neighborhoods are very unfriendly and that one could live on a street for a year without talking to a soul. Maybe carrying a petition is one way to gain friends and influence people. Out of these eight families, there was an Army captain, one scientist, one man with a good position in the department store, an ex-professor connected with CBS, a woman working for Tennessee Eastman Corporation as a counselor—so you can see how difficult it would be for any of them to get to know each other socially.

I saw a car driven by a chauffeur for the first time since I came here. They were obviously not from the "area," because they asked me directions to the Guest House.

One of the first questions people ask you here is "what does your husband do?" As one woman said, "It's so much easier to catalogue people that way."

Whenever you make a purchase, the salespeople invariably say, "Thank you, come back." Snuff is a good seller here.

I have an extra copy of the Oak Ridge Journal which I am sending you. Until security was lifted here, no names were ever mentioned in the paper. To quote an early edition "that owing to, shall we say, space . . . the Journal cannot print the names of any persons in its columns for the present. This will explain our failure to publish various news items contributed—we are unique—the only newspaper in the country without any news." When they announced the first baby born in Oak Ridge, just the first name was given— no last name or address. During the war, visitors were limited to entering through only two gates. The paper has always been and still is delivered to every resident here via the postman. I think it is read by almost everyone, especially the classified ads. It is supported by the Recreation and Welfare Association, and these expenses are $37,000 a year. The only revenue that the paper gets are the ads.

The Rec and Welfare—as it is called—had a meeting last week to report of past, present and future activitities. All citizens were invited. The meeting was at the high school, where most important meetings take place, and I was shocked to find only about fifty people in the audience. Anyway, I learned many interesting things. Representatives from Carbide, T.E.C., Clinton Lab and the Army met soon after Oak Ridge was built to make a survey of the recreational need.

At that time the population was 5,000, and as the city grew, R&W broadened the activities. They were responsible to the Army, but were allowed to run things for profit. These profits went back into the fund to provide further recreational acitivities. They collected quite a sum from the movies, concessions for amusement, and sale of beer. With this they support the orchestras, library, paid for books and librarian, ball fields, halls, and they now sponsor over seventy clubs—all organizations must be approved by R&W— and picnic areas. There are 10,000 people registered in the library and they have a traveling library for people in the hutment area. There are 36 to 40 activities for adults, including croquet, weight-lifting, boxing, basketball. There are 125 softball teams and one in seventeen residents plays softball. One of the problems is to provide enough recreation to meet the 40-hour week. Dancing is the most popular entertainment here, particularly square dancing. There is a further account in the Journal.

The Kiwanis has called representatives of all groups here to make plans for the Overseas Famine Relief. I have been asked to become a member of the board of directors. Ho hum, jobs are piling up for me, but this is one I can't refuse. Sometimes I do wish I were two people, though, so I could divide my activities among me. Now, poor Dick has to eat all of Irene's leftovers. You can't just throw away a jar of strained apricots and farina. I am looking forward to the peace and quiet of New York when we have our vacation in August. Mama says it's time for bed.

> G'night.
> [sig] Thelma

Ruth and Milton Carey and their six-year-old child came to Oak Ridge when Ruth was twenty-two. Perhaps because she had an older child she became, as others have said, almost a mother to many of those she met. But her involvements were more than social. I asked her if she had been connected with the informal starts of recreational activities such as the orchestra and the art museum. Her reply:

> We have always supported those things. I was one of the founders of the art thing, and I'll tell you how it began.
>
> We always had a good time, and we were at a party one night that was given by two bachelors and they said, "We're going to have an Irish wake." Why? "Because there has never been one here before."
>
> They made a dummy out of clothes and put it in the bathtub with ice around it, and there were watermelons in there on the ice, too. It was just a real crazy, fun party, and we were dancing. There was a man named Gil Frederickson whom I had never met, and I remember dancing with him. We got into a small-talk conversation like "I like to paint. I like art," that kind of thing.
>
> He said, "Is there an art center here?" I told him, "No." (I had been in a group which included the wife of a well-known scientist and we used to get together at different homes, just a bunch of women with young children, to paint, but there was no formal art organization.)
>
> Then he said, "Let's form one," and I said, "OK," and forgot all about it.
>
> But he called me the next day and said, "Well, I'm ready to start the art group. Do you know a lot of people who are interested in art?"
>
> I said, "Yes, I do."
>
> "Well, invite them. I need to have them at a meeting at my house tonight." And I said, "OK."
>
> A lot of them came, and there was a second meeting about a week later. This was not too long after I went to work in 1948; and I remember he called me at the office, and I remember wondering "Should I go to his house?" I did, and I was very glad. Of course, there were other people who were much more involved, who gave it a lot more than I did. They did a tremendous amount of work. I just happened to be there at the time.

More reaction to Oak Ridge's unique social structure:

A fairly new arrival—who came here in the late 1950s—told me that she still considers herself a newcomer, and therefore an outsider. Occasionally she and her husband have the privilege of meeting socially with some of the pioneers, and she said that she can't hear enough of the early days. However, she laments that she can never penetrate and be a part of the closed circle of the IN group, and she envies their having had those once-in-a-lifetime experiences.

Then there was a nurse, whose husband accepted a position as a chemist in one of the labs in 1961. They had been living in Paducah, Kentucky. After spending a few weeks in Oak Ridge looking around and meeting the people with the prospect of settling there, they decided to live in Knoxville. Aside from seeing the city as "big, dirty and sprawling with blocks of houses all alike, they found the atmosphere in Oak Ridge too cosmopolitan and the people too 'uppity.'"

Pre-fab homes were put up in a matter of days. Photo by Ed Wescott. Courtesy Department of Energy

Pre-fab units were shipped into Oak Ridge by the hundreds. Photo by Ed Wescott. Courtesy Department of Energy

Pre-fab housing construction. Photo by Ed Wescott. Courtesy Department of Energy

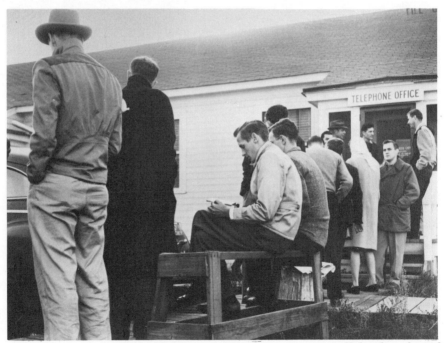

For early residents of Oak Ridge, waiting in line was a way of life. Photo by Ed Wescott. Courtesy Department of Energy

The Oak Ridge Symphony, composed of scientists, doctors, teachers, house-wives, and anyone interested in music, with Waldo Cohn conducting, was one of the first attempts to enrich the cultural lives of Oak Ridgers. Photo by Ed Wescott. Courtesy Department of Energy.

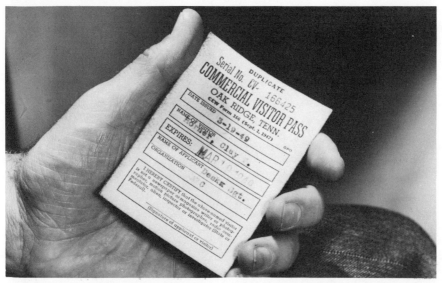

Even though the war had ended, residents and visitors alike still had to put up with the inconveniences of living in a still somewhat closed and hush-hush atmosphere, predominated by military secrecy. Passes were required well into the 1950's. Photo by Ed Wescott. Courtesy Department of Energy.

Our first week in Oak Ridge was spent in the Guest House, about the only structure in the community set up to accommodate visitors and newcomers. Motels and hotels were non-existent. For many young mothers, the only form of entertainment was rocking away the hours on the front porch of the Guest House. The building still stands today as the Alexander Hotel. Photo by Ed Wescott. Courtesy Department of Energy.

Many laborers were put up in small trailer units. During the peak war years, 7,000 trailers were brought in for housing. Photo by Ed Wescott. Courtesy Department of Energy

The families of black laborers were confined to an area consisting of sub-standard housing known as "hutments." Photo by Ed Wescott. Courtesy Department of Energy

Many of our single friends spent their early years in Oak Ridge in dormitories like these. The dream of many was to move into single-unit family housing. Photo by Ed Wescott. Courtesy Department of Energy.

Our friends the Coveyous lived in an efficiency apartment like this. Each structure was composed of four family units. Photo by Ed Wescott. Courtesy Department of Energy.

Junior scientists and GI families lived in cracker box-like "Victory Cottages," which housed two families each. Photo by Ed Westcott. Courtesy Department of Energy.

Letter IX

Dear Margaret,

Last Friday, for the first time in the ten weeks that I have been in Oak Ridge, I left the "area" for the "outside" and "civilization." I hadn't realized how long I had been penned up, and had a magnificent sense of freedom and adventure as soon as the bus went through the gate.

First of all, seeing houses made of brick and wood with gables and hedges—houses that seemed so substantial compared to our cemesto board and demountables—just thrilled me. I felt as if I wanted to dig my teeth into them. Then shopping in Knoxville in big, air-conditioned department stores where I was actually able to buy things that I wanted. And to top it all, lunch at Walgreen's, where I sat at the counter and almost believed I was "back home."

On the way back, I held up the busload for several minutes (feeling like an idiot) because I had to rummage through all my bundles to find my badge. Must say the MP was very patient.

Sunday afternoon was another new experience in Oak Ridge. We were invited to a tea for the University of Tennessee faculty. I wore a hat and gloves! We were driven there by another prof and his wife from Knoxville. They used the tea as an excuse to look over our town with the view of moving here, but the wife turned up her nose at us. She didn't like the fact that some of the houses face the backs of other houses. I found myself bristling at some of her questions and disdainful manner, and realized that I have developed quite a lot of civic pride without being aware of it.

Some friends took us out Saturday afternoon to show Mother the sights and sites of Oak Ridge. We passed a new section of prefabs that had been flat,

91

empty land five months ago. There seemed to be a thousand houses there. And, most curious of all, we already have a "ghost town" here. This was a community that had been called Wheat Town or Happy Valley, and before it closed down about October, the construction workers of K-25 lived here. The inhabitants needed a separate pass to live there and were not permitted to come into Oak Ridge proper without a special pass. Conversely, Oak Ridgians could not go there without a special permit. The people there also needed further identification to enter the plant. This was, I believe, the only community here where white and colored lived in close relationship. But, of course, the colored community was segregated. Passing there now and seeing row upon row of empty trailers, hutments, barracks, empty stores, cafeteria, post office with not a soul around—except ghosts—and these structures already starting to decay and sag is a most depressing sight indeed. If I hadn't stupidly forgotten my badge again, we could have gone "outside" and seen more of the wonderful Cumberland hills. I see now that it is important to have it at all times, especially when driving. But for my carelessness, a whole carful of people were confined to Oak Ridge.

I was surprised to discover recently that the Red Cross has many occasions to give loans to destitute families or individuals here. This, of course, is a general custom of the RC, but because all of the people who live here must also work here, I assumed there was no unemployment or real poverty. But in the trailer camps, particularly, there are many typical cases. A worker will desert his wife and family and disappear. The wife is left alone to pay rent ($15 a month for a single trailer and $20 for a double with the sixth month rent-free), feed and clothe children, on no income. There are many widows with children who came here to work. Many have become ill and need hospitalization. Or the father who is the sole support of the family will be out of work for a long period, and soon savings are all used up for medical expenses and convalescence. A lot of them are too proud or ignorant to find out what their rights are or are overlooking taking necessary precautions such as insurance, and are not eligible for compensations. Then, too, there are layoffs.

Remember I once mentioned that there is a community of colored, married people living in victory cottages right near the colored hutment camp? Well, it is only five months since Negro families were permitted to live on the area. Those cottages were inhabited formerly by white construction workers. One of the reasons that colored families hesitate moving here is the lack of recreational facilities. They can't go to any of the movies here or take advantage of anything except what they have in the camp. Wonder what the CIO will do for the Negroes when it gets going? I am sending you some of the literature of their beginnings here. Also wonder what influence the DAR has here.

Oak Ridge is being painted. Sometimes while on a bus, I see a group of about ten houses with men in white climbing all over them with their paint brushes. It looks like a cartoon of something. There has been a little trouble, however. It seems as if the contracts were made with two companies, and one doesn't want to play. So there are gripes from many residents who have been here for years who aren't being done, while a newcomer gets all prettied up.

Poor Dick had to come home today without his coat jacket. He shares a hutment with a roommate at the lab, and his RM locked the door, which has a special lock, while Dick was out. His badge was in his pocket and also a notebook containing the combination to the lock. So he had a special military escort drive him past the gate. And now he has to get a temporary pass to get in again. Ah, regulations!

Oak Ridge has a little "Westchester." It's real swanky and is called "Nob Hill." You have to be a least an Army colonel to live there. The wives and pretty blonde children loll about on their lawns all day in spiffy clothes.

About hats here. Don't be misled by a picture in the Oak Ridge Journal of a group of women in spring bonnets. The hats were for the photographer's benefit. One man saw the picture and didn't recognize one woman he knows extremely well. His wife explained he had never seen her in a hat.

Oh yes, and about the painting—most people I talk to are apathetic about it. A typical comment is: "We hate to go through the mess. Might only be here six months." One woman who made a similiar remark added that she had been saying that for three years and may be saying it three years from now.

We have not given up hopes about getting a car. I have read the series in the Herald Tribune on the automobile situation—so I suppose Knoxville isn't entirely to blame. We had a wonderful opportunity to get a 1941 Ford with the front fender all bashed in—and a coupe at that—for $1,250. There are loads of Oak Ridge people with a little knowledge of mechanics who buy up cars, slobber some paint on them and get those fancy prices. But, who knows, we may come rolling into New York even if it's only on one tire.

Do you recommend "Sociology Principles and Problems" by Ellwood? It is the only book on that subject in the library, but perhaps there is something better that you would advise. I have taken it out, plus "Prairie City." Now to read a little and so to bed.

Hope this "little" note finds you and the family in the best of health.

    As ever,

[sig] Thelma

My troubles with passes were not reflected in the experiences of Shirley Brooks—to whom a hole in the famed fence was a way to avoid a long walk to enter Oak Ridge legally. She told me of her early days living in a boxcar just outside the city:

I arrived in Oak Ridge in 1943 when I was eight years old. My daddy worked for the Louisville & Nashville Railroad and was sent there to receive freight when they were constructing the town. We moved from Williamsburg, Kentucky, where my father had started working when he left the coal mining camp in Gatliff. We lived right by the railroad tracks at a place called Elza Gate. There was no housing available for the railroad people, so the L&N ran a spur track off the main track right next to the limits of Oak Ridge.

Then they brought in six or seven boxcars and converted them into three rooms each. We had one boxcar per family. They had a kitchen at one end; the middle part was the living room; and at the other end was a bedroom. The middle part of the car had big double windows on each side and a door. From the door there were seventeen steps to the ground outside. They had a closet into the bedroom and, at the other end of the car, a closet on each side. They were nice. We had no running water for toilet facilities or sinks. We had to carry all the water we used from a well which was in a nearby trailer camp on the railroad property. There was a counter in the kitchen, and I remember that we always had to wash dishes in a dishpan on the kitchen table. I had a friend who thought it was so exotic to have an outdoor bathroom. When I had her to a slumber party one night, she got the "call" about 2 A.M. I handed her the flashlight and said, "Here, there's the path." She didn't think it was such a great thing after that.

Most of the people who lived in the boxcars were clerks, like Daddy, and operators. Even the agent for the railroad lived in one. Our family consisted of my father, mother, me, two older brothers and one grandmother (sometimes two).

We used to have a lot of relatives coming down from Kentucky to see about getting work in Oak Ridge, and they'd stay with us. Also, a lot of relatives moved down here. Once sixteen spent the night with us, and we only had three sleeping on the floor, which was a miracle!

Because we were so close to the railroad track, it was terribly noisy when a train went by. But we were accustomed to it, and it never bothered us. But one hot summer night an out-of-town couple was sleeping in the bedroom with the door open. A train had crossed the bridge and was coming around the curve. It looked as if it was approaching straight into the room. The woman jumped up, grabbed her husband and yelled, "God, Morris, it's coming right in here with us!"

After a while, Daddy built what we called a "room-on-the-ground." We'd walk down the seventeen steps from the boxcar to that room. Then he built more rooms around it, using the first one as the core. He used to bring home the big packing cases that things arrived in and that he'd unpacked. He'd just stand them up and there'd be a wall or a side of a room. My parents lived in that house for, I guess, thirty years. They finally had to vacate, and it was taken away from their property.

It didn't bother me at all that we didn't live in a house inside Oak Ridge. Most of the people who lived close to where we were lived in the large trailer camp. We had a lot of contact with them and got to know them—especially since we used their well for water. We had more room than they did, and I don't recall any resentment at all. It was just that they lived in one kind of a house and we lived in another. I enjoyed going home from school with my friends, and they enjoyed coming to my house, too. So it was always an adventure. I used to sleepwalk when we lived in that boxcar, and one of the neighbors would take me home and put me back to bed. Then she'd wake my mother and say, "Well, she's been out again!"

I sort of grew up in and out of Oak Ridge. We had to have passes to get in.

We didn't want to walk from our house all the way to Elza Gate, so we used to go through the fence where there was a gap. But we always made sure that we had a valid pass, and never went in unless we had one. We went into Oak Ridge a lot through the fence to go to the movies, do our shopping, and things like that.

But I couldn't go to school in Oak Ridge, since we were outside the city limits. I had to go to a little place in the county for elementary school. Then I went to high school in Clinton and graduated from there. However, one of my brothers went to Oak Ridge High School. He was able to get in because he was supposed to be living with a cousin there at the time.

There was some jealousy because we always felt that the Oak Ridge schools had such better facilities and could offer so many more different courses than the county schools could. There was just not as much money in the county as in Oak Ridge to spend on schools. So there was some envy on that level. I was editor of our high school paper in Clinton, and we went into Oak Ridge occasionally to visit their paper. Our contacts with the children were through sports. In fact, there was a lot of rivalry between Oak Ridge teams and the towns outside. The football teams had some royal battles.

One of my biggest treats was a trip to Knoxville. Mother and I would take the bus at Elza Gate. We'd go the Mid-Day Merry-Go-Round and then to Kress's and have oysters—always oysters. It was delightful. I loved riding the tandem buses, which were in two sections.

The one thing I remember about the war is the day President Roosevelt died. I was in the living room with my mother, and we heard it on the radio. Mother was so upset; she went out on the little front porch and looked around for someone else to talk to. She was crying.

When the bombs were dropped on Japan, everybody said, "Oh, well, I knew what they were doing all along." Of course nobody really knew but they claimed that they did. But I think a lot of people suspicioned something.

Later came the big whoop-de-do on the opening up of Oak Ridge with all the celebrities coming in and the big crowds at the gate. It was really something!

After high school I worked in Clinton for two-and-a-half years and then went to work at the Lab in Oak Ridge as a secretary. I got married in 1957. My husband was a graduate student at the University of Tennessee. I worked at the Lab for five years and then left when I was about to give birth to my first baby.

Just after the war, the railroad took the boxcars away. I don't know why, except that somebody remembered that they were there. By that time, our house was finished, and my parents stayed there until about 1975. Then when all the derailments started happening, the railroad got really scared and decided that they had to get the places so close to the tracks away from there. Daddy had already retired, so they moved into Oak Ridge and still live there. They had been there so long watching the city grow, they had put their roots down. They had no more close ties in Kentucky and would not have gone back there. They thought Knoxville was too big. All their friends were in Oak Ridge. It was a good central location. It was home.

Every once in a while, we'd see our old boxcar sitting somewhere for one of the section hands to use. The railroad used them for years after they took them away, everywhere—up and down into Kentucky, around Tennessee, on the Corbin end of the line mostly. But we'd see our number on it and recognize it as being "our" car.

I was not alone in my trials with passes at the Oak Ridge gates. C.O. Moak, writing in the *Oak Ridge National Laboratory Review* in 1946, had two amusing paragraphs on the tribulations of others:

To go from Knoxville to work, I had to pass through four perimeter checkpoints; from Oak Ridge, three. The guards were partly soldiers, partly civilians. Some gates had Geiger counters, and sometimes we'd put a penny in the reactor and plant it on some poor sucker as he went hurrying out to catch his bus home. The day I arrived, in August 1944, John Brolley was taking a bath under the fire shower in the hall of the Physics Building, because he'd been stacking graphite all day and looked like a coal miner. He had a fine singing voice. The halls got pretty wet.

One day the head of the Manhattan Engineer District, General L. R. Groves, was scheduled to visit the Laboratory. At the time, I happened to be in the office of the director, M. D. Whitaker, in the administration building overlooking the front gate. The general's car and entourage came to the gate and went through. After passing the gate about fifty feet, General Groves got out of his car and walked back to the gate to give the GI guard hell for not asking for his badge. What GI would have ever asked for the General's badge?

Letter X

Oak Ridge, Tenn.
June 6, 1946

Dear Margaret,

I have just been sitting on the porch and gazing at our "new" car, a 1939 Plymouth. Until either or both Dick and I learn to drive it, we shall have to be content with the pleasure of looking at it and knowing it is ours. Irene and I have been practicing getting in and out. Great fun.

Decoration Day was a peculiar holiday here. All of the stores, schools and companies controlled or run by Southerners went about their business as usual. The few Northern companies celebrated by closing—so some Southerners working for Northern companies celebrated for the first time, and Northerners working for Southern companies didn't celebrate it for the first time.

I realized that Ellwood was pretty stuffy after reading a little of it. Would appreciate "Yankee City" very much.

There has been a lot of excitement in Oak Ridge since the CIO has started organizing, and we are all interested in the contest between them and the AFL—and the outcome. I haven't seen any literature or handouts from the AFL, except newspaper accounts, but the CIO is doing a remarkable job in making Oak Ridge aware of them. I have no doubt that the whole South is waiting to see what happens here.

I have a friend who is counselor to girls at one of the big companies, and she has many interesting stories to tell. Just recently, she was called upon to investigate a pregnant, unmarried worker. She has had several cases like that. She doesn't attribute this especially to youth or "badness", although in some instances nice, innocent girls were thrown in with pretty fast ones. But the main thing is that most of the people have the attitude that nobody knows them here and they can get away with lots of things that they wouldn't dream of doing in their own hometown. A young girl we knew from New York was asked to take a job here, and it interested her very much, but she came for a few days to look over the housing. About the only provisions for single people living here is a dorm. We looked at a few, and I can understand now why such things happen.

There are hundreds of these dorms—girls and men have separate ones. There is only one with rooms having adjoining baths. The rest have tiny, untidy and dirty rooms without even washstands. Girls walk around the corridors in various stages of undress, with no privacy. I know that living conditions like that are not peculiar to Oak Ridge. For example, New York has many places like that and even worse, but here there is hardly any possibility for men and women to live in a homelike environment no matter what the income. There is some talk of converting some dorms to small apartments, but no one knows if or when young people will be eligible.

Incidentally, the Army still has complete overall control of housing. Each company has an allotment of houses for their personnel, and there are new rules constantly about distribution, plus the usual red tape. It is all very vague, and I believe it helps to know the right people.

Talking about rules, people still must be cleared before they can come here to work. In some ways "they" seem to be tightening up, and the latest rule is that a month is required for clearance. This also applies to anyone coming here for an interview. Some think it is because of the Canadian spy scare.

I have met several people working for social agencies, including the Red Cross. There are five different social agencies here, and they are all kept quite busy. According to one RC worker, Oak Ridge is the only city where the RC has been allotted a fund for helping out local indigents and home relief. They have been overburdened with work and handle from 250 to 275 cases a month. They handle the care of unmarried pregnant girls—and, as I have mentioned, there has been an inordinate number. An interesting sidelight is that a great many of the residents here have requested these babies for adoption. But they have to get them through the regular agencies. (Incidentally, the laws for adoption in the state of Tennessee are very lax. One can adopt a baby in twenty-four hours without any investigation. The state chapters of the League of Women Voters are working to amend these laws.)

A chapter of the League is in formation in Oak Ridge, and part of the program will be to investigate social problems. I shall probably be active in the organization, as well as representatives of many groups, including the RC, social workers, Army wives, teacher groups, etc. And I expect, through it, my education on Oak Ridge will go much deeper.

You say that Oak Ridge has been pointed out as a perfect community. For my part, I should hate to think so or that this is anyone's idea of a model city. Physically, the residential section has been planned very carefully and in many respects is ideal. At any rate, it forms an excellent basis for the future. And if the plan is to eliminate eventually the trailer camps, hutments, crowded prefab sections and slum areas—well, maybe. But from a social viewpoint, there is little in its favor.

At present, with the Army still in control, everyone is filled with uncertainty about the future. Some say that they [the Army] will soon pull out, and others are not so sure. Everybody hopes so. A group of people are just forming a Good Government League, and the idea is to study all types of city government and to be ready with a plan when the time comes. This whole subject really requires a great deal of knowledge and background of Oak Ridge. Having been here such a short time, I feel that what I have discovered so far is still superficial and I haven't begun to scratch the surface. However, this place fascinates me so much that I want to keep digging till I reach bottom.

There are many things that I would love to tell you, but it would take pages and pages. We plan on being in New York for about a month starting about the middle of August. We hope you will be in town sometime during our stay.

Dick is leaving for Chicago Sunday for a week. It has been very hot, and we have a houseful of company this week; so I have been writing this letter between washing dishes, serving cold drinks and trying to bake a bread pudding, which got so burnt that Irene called it "caviar." But I want to get this off before you leave for the country and to wish you a pleasant summer. Dick says, "Me too."

As ever,
[sig] Thelma

"Briarfield"
R.F.D. 1
Ashland, N.H.

July 19, 1946

Dear Thelma,

I've had a lot of small casualties, a hurt foot, a cut hand, which have complicated life to the point where letters have been very difficult—and not much work has been done. But don't let that discourage you. I will see that "Yankee City" is sent you when I go down to New York next week.

Yours,
[sig] Margaret

Even for married women, pregnancy in Oak Ridge was something of an adventure. Kathryn Cantrell tells of the experiences of three young women she knew:

Harriet and her young husband settled in their first home, an efficiency apartment. They came in the spring of '44. They were very happy in that situation, though they didn't like the mud one day and the dust the next. There was never anything in between. Always just mud or dust. And they didn't like the long lines at the grocery store. But they were content at first in their efficiency apartment.

Later when the flattops were available to them, they decided they needed a little more space and so they moved. In '45, they were expecting their first child. The war was going well and, as it appeared that it would be over very soon, they assumed that they would be leaving Oak Ridge. So they thought it wise not to buy baby furniture. They were confident that they would be away from Oak Ridge before the baby was born. But the war was over, they were still here, and the baby was born. So their first-born went home only to sleep in the drawer of one of the chests of drawers in their flattop.

Linda another young woman I knew, came to Oak Ridge in April of '44. Her fiancé had come in '43. He went back to Mississippi in April; they were married and came directly to Oak Ridge. She remembers thinking—as she came through the gate at the top of the hill from Oliver Springs—"The mail will never find me here. I am at the end of civilization!" They, too, had a one-room efficiency apartment at first, but she was most unhappy. Her husband worked long hours, and she was lonely.

In the fall she took a job at the Oak Ridge Hospital that kept her busy, and she was more content. In November of '45, she went to the hospital for the birth of their first child. She was greeted at the door of the labor room by a nurse who said, "Oh, no! Not another one!" They had already delivered thirteen babies on that shift.

Linda was in labor for thirty-two hours, had a difficult delivery, and, when her baby was finally born, he had to be clad in a torn shirt that was fastened together with a big safety pin. He, too, had to sleep in a drawer in the nursery at the hospital. Linda was surprised to find herself in a private room after the delivery: the usual thing was a six-bed ward. The nurse told her that they had prepared the room for General [Leslie R.] Groves, but that he hadn't shown up. So they gave it to her since she had had such a hard time. General Groves was the No. 1 man with the army and wasn't in town always, and I am told that when he was there, he very often slept in the maternity ward at the hospital, because, that way, nobody could find him.

Another young woman, Marie, had been married six months when she and her groom came to Oak Ridge. Her husband had been told when he was hired by Tennessee Eastman that he would be working at the Clinton Engineer Works, and also had been told to report at the Tennessee Eastman Employment Office in Knoxville.

As they drove south—just south of LaFollette—they began to see signs for Clinton. So they thought, "Oh, that must be where the Clinton Engineer Works are." Her husband had been told that at this particular job, they were doing exciting new research. When they got to Clinton, they didn't think that that looked like a town where exciting new research was going on; but they went on to Knoxville and were further puzzled by what they were told there. They were told that they would live in Oak Ridge, which was a town that was not yet on the map. They, like others, were assigned a one-room apartment for a while, but eventually were assigned a flattop.

When their first child was born in mid-December of that year, Marie was to go home from the hospital on the twenty-third. Her husband came by the hospital after work, and checked her and the baby out. When he went to the parking lot to get their car, it wouldn't start. It took considerable time to repair it. It was dark and the baby was crying when they got home to their flattop. They were anxious to get in the door—but not for long. When they opened it, they were met by billows of smoke. The husband had attempted to stoke the heater so that the fire would hold all day and it would be nice and warm when they got there that night.

But he had put in too much coal dust—we had to use a great deal of it in those days—on a hot fire and had all but smothered it out. When it did burn through, it did it with such force that it blew the stove door open. It had smoked every nook and cranny of the house, and spewed fine silt-like ashes out the bottom which covered everything.

But being pregnant was not without its advantages. Lothar W. Nordheim wrote in the Fall 1976 of the *Oak Ridge National Laboratory Review:*

> When housing became available in January 1944, we took up residence at Oak Ridge and lived through the usual experiences of all early inhabitants. Your feet were apt to stick in the mud while your head choked in the dust. You had to learn to shovel coal and to bank the furnace for the night. You felt quite isolated, even within the reservation with the tight security barriers between the various sites.
>
> From a long-range point of view, this isolation was not a real disadvantage, for we each had to learn to solve our own problems. Also we developed a spirit of comradeship and helped one another. Close, enduring friendships were made easily. We were all in the same boat.
>
> The long working days were not made shorter by the bumpy rides to the distant lab. But they were not without their amusing incidents. One day on the bus, my wife [Gertrude], then visibily pregnant, engaged in a spirited discussion with Charles Coryell. She mentioned the element rhenium, and the guard thought she had said "uranium." Due to her delicate condition she got away with mild reprimand, but not until she had been given a lengthy exhortation in my presence.

K.Z. Morgan told another tale of dust, also in the same issue of the *ORNL Review:*

> In the early days, Clinton Laboratories issued employees knee boots as part of our essential equipment. One day as we left the cafeteria (fifty yards east of the present west gate), we heard a plaintive cry, and looking around, we saw Frances Bishop, a health physics technician, into mud above her knees. We got boards and made our way out to her. By pulling from the front and pushing from the rear, we finally extracted her, but her boots were left buried knee-deep where they remain to this day—now of course under the hard-surface main laboratory road.

Letter XI

Oak Ridge, Tenn.
July 27, 1946

Dear Margaret,

I have been going at a whirlwind pace for several weeks and have about come up for breath. Local politics have always seemed remote to me, but somehow I became terribly involved. I was put on the Good Government Committee of the League of Women Voters, then the chairman got sick and the whole works were thrown in my lap. Well, I learned a lot.

I think I mentioned that a Good Government Group was in formation here. I was a representative to one of the meetings to which came representatives from over twenty civic and fraternal clubs in the area. There were Eagles, Elks and Lions, as well as the Rotary, Kiwanis, Masons and Eastern Star. Everyone was very fraternal; no one wore hoods; and nothing was accomplished.

The CIO has been throwing a lot of bombshells in Oak Ridge. They have made several accusations about the way things are being run here that no one has dared to express openly. Their weekly paper is distributed to everyone and has become quite a topic of conversation. And it doesn't take long to discover who is for and who's agin it. And it is amazing how consistent people are—referring to Northerners and Southerners. Unfortunately, while most of their charges are true, they [CIO] have been a little careless with some facts, and that leaves them open to attack. However, they have forced the Oak Ridge Journal to come out with long articles of explanation.

The people here are beginning to feel that it is about time they are treated as any other citizens. They want to feel they can ask why, how and where, and have a voice and a right to criticize. Many people honestly believe we have a dictatorship here. It isn't that living here is unpleasant; I guess it has some-

103

thing to do with regimentation. It is also a nuisance to have to ask permission for almost anything.

We would like to know about concessions, for one thing. Why is it so difficult for some people to have a small business here? Why are prices higher here than in surrounding communities? What is the real story on the only department store quitting Oak Ridge? Why can't medical men be permitted to practice outside of the hospital, instead of patients having to pay regular office fees in clinic surroundings?

Then there is a long list of gripes from the dormitory dwellers. Their conditions are so distasteful that a vacation custom has developed here. Most of the people living in permanent homes invite single men and women to live in their houses while they are away. In our case, two young girls are going to live here while we are gone. Lots of young people can knock out a whole summer escaping the dorms and gypsying from one house to another.

Oak Ridge is a happy hunting ground for rackets. Since shopping is so limited and scarce items even scarcer, people get taken in. It works two ways. First, there are people living here who are fed stuff from contacts "outside." They can work up quite a business getting customers here. As you know, no salesman can get in here. People who have "terminated" keep up with their old friends here, get passes when they want them, and in an afternoon can make a pretty penny on nylons, etc. Then there are complete outsiders who will pick up an acquaintance with people on the buses living here. They will get them interested in whatever they have to sell and get them to take orders for it among their friends. They might arrange for them to get a pass to come in or meet outside at some appointed spot for the exchange of money and merchandise. Incidentally, this occurs mostly among young girls. The house-wife usually doesn't get around so much, and is perhaps not so gullible.

The painters have been crawling all over us for more than a week—and that is only for the outside of the house. We have had four different crews so far. One for the first coat of green on the frame of the house and one for the first coat of darker green for the doors. Then each one for the second coats of light and dark green. Then we expect two more for the windows and also for the porch floor. Some sixteen altogether plus innumerable foremen and super-visors. I understand the inside job can go on for weeks.

Oak Ridge is going to be a big force in Tennessee politics. For one thing, it is the fifth-largest city in the state. We hold more than half the votes (according to poll tax receipts) in the county. Most of the people have been living here long enough to vote, and there are nine men from Oak Ridge running for county offices. All but five states in the country are represented here.

I was interested in getting some facts about the activities of the Red Cross, and spoke to one of the head workers. (She was giving me some driving lessons.) But no reports have been published, and it would be impossible to get any official information. I do know that all of the social agencies are understaffed, and most of the people are overworked.

You won't believe it when I tell you that I have been making my own butter. What with berries and fruits so plentiful—Dick and Irene picked a half pail of blackberries one morning—everybody is busy with canning and making jellies. It makes it hard for us city gals. I balked at jelly-making, but a friend of mine who lives between two country housewives was made to feel like a parasite. She called me tearfully one night at 10:30 and was still struggling with jars and caps. It was hot and she was exhausted, and the sad part was that she didn't even like peaches. I really got away with murder the night we attended a community supper. Each of the four couples was assigned to bring part of the meal. We were the vegetables. Thank the Lord for Bird's Eye. Dick's comment—after eating homemade bread, wonderful roast beef and homemade cake, punch and salad—was "no need to guess who brought the vegetables." I still think he was being a little mean.

The first time we used the car, we discovered a leak in the gas tank. Dick said we were getting twenty gallons to the mile. A few days later we were stalled on the highway and had to be towed to a garage. Then we had a fire and fortunately an MP came by and we had the whole Oak Ridge fire department out, but what worried us most that time was that neither of us had our license. Anyway, we still hope it will get us to New York.

I hope all your complications are gone, and you are all having a cool, pleasant summer.

Best wishes,
[sig] Thelma

In 1980, I thought back on how we got that first car and our early experiences with it:

The *Oak Ridge Journal*[1] had one feature that was widely and avidly read—the Ad Column. It was a valuable asset to newcomers who needed things hard to come by, and to those leaving the area and who wanted to cash in on some of the possessions they had to leave behind.

When I spied an ad, "For sale, Plymouth, '39, excellent condition, call . . .," my hopes rose. I called the listed number and the owner drove over right away. The Plymouth was no beauty, especially at the exorbitant asking price of $350, but the man assured us it had been thoroughly overhauled and had gone only 50,000 miles.

Neither of us had ever driven a car or knew anything about the mechanics of an automobile. However, we were desperate. New cars were not yet in production, and, even if they had been, we would have felt out of place with one in Oak Ridge. Everyone who had a car—no matter how old and battered—was holding on to it.

With a trip to New York looming a month away, we were ready to settle for anything that would get us from here to there. We bought the car on sight. It was to be our "Magic Carpet."

---

[1] For an account of journalism in Oak Ridge, see an article by June Adamson, "From Bulletin to Broadside: A History of By-Authority Journalism in Oak Ridge, Tennessee," *Tennessee Historical Quarterly*, XXXVIII (1979), 479-93.

Dick, at least, needed to get his driver's license as soon as possible; and friends gave him lessons after work and one weekend. Knoxville was the nearest city to take the driver's test. Still, Dick was not absolutely confident. That's why we sneaked out one night, when traffic was light, for extra practice. And that's when the smoke started oozing from the hood. It happened right at Elza Gate. We were grateful to the MPs for their help; but petrified when a policeman arrived soon after. He had a three-page form to be filled out, and by the time we answered all the questions, he could have written our biographies. We didn't dare look at each other while waiting for that fateful question, "Let's see your driver's license." He never asked us. Our fears were needless, because at that time policemen were not permitted to make arrests in Oak Ridge. After that night, our Magic Carpet was renamed "Thelma's Folly."

Helen Jernigen also found out about rackets in Oak Ridge, as she remembered in her interview:

I worked in a recreation hall for an individual who operated a duckpin alley, a bowling alley and the theater. The recreation hall did a lively business in black-market cigarettes, although I didn't know that at the time. It was sort of a carnival-like, large place with games. You shot at things, and you shot baskets, and the prizes were always cigarettes. It never dawned on poor, naive me that I was involved in crime till afterwards when the FBI came and closed it down after the summer was over.

I was safely back in college by then, and felt as if I had made the whole experience up. I didn't know I had been in Oak Ridge. I told people that I lived in Happy Valley. Later, I began to think probably it was Clinton, so I began to say I worked in Clinton. Not until some time later did I realize I had been in the very early Oak Ridge.

The next year I came back and started work at K-25, now completed, again in a recreation place, but this time a legitimate one.

Change, as my letters to Margaret showed, came to Oak Ridge in many ways. The differences and conflicts between people from widely different backgrounds were muffled but not hidden by wartime urgency, and became more apparent as the city became more normal. Lydia Bredig, the psychologist, commented on these both in a lecture in 1980 and in an interview with me that same year. The gist of her remarks:

Another aspect emphasizing the differences is that the institutions which a lot of the men and women had before were not here in Oak Ridge.

Families from different disciplines lived close together. A lot of the country families met the wives of scientists and some of their husbands, and other women who were working here in one way or another, and some who were single. But the community of women became closer across cultural levels—particularly when children came.

All people working here absorbed the conviction that what they were doing was crucially important, whether they knew the nature of that mission or not. But the sense of partaking in a mission was basically unquestioned, and no matter what you did, somebody depended on you and counted on you. So people got to know each other at work, as neighbors, and in fun. During this time, they tended to idealize each other very intensely in terms of wisdom, knowledge, habits and goals. It made for great intensity of feelings, of great love, and of great admiration. And when these ideals could not be met, anger, derision, and rejection became as intense.

So what we had was an idealization of two different groups that were coming together and then polarization of real anger because, certainly, nobody could possibly have met these ideals. What happened then was that the long-haired, the scientific and technical groups were deemed dreamers, foolish professors out of school and practical idiots. Some long-hairs saw the outlanders as crude buffoons, devoid of sensitivity, and out to cheat you. Thus they met, they loved each other, they fought, they sang together, and acquired each other's values. What emerged was an onsurge of exuberance, renewed adolescence, and a push of activity and creativity in many directions. The theoretical physicist gardened and played piano. The chemist painted and made wine. Some hunted, built houses, learned different languages and scientific lore—and what emerged was well toward becoming the Renaissance man, working and accomplishing in diverse ways. In this ebb and flow of interchange, most people returned to the basic values of their early culture.

Now the women in Oak Ridge have been known in many circles outside of Oak Ridge as rather special. The process of becoming special was somehow different from that of their men. During the early years, the single, unmarried women—except for teachers—tended to identify themselves with the working male, since most of them were working for men. Their roles, with few exceptions, were helping roles—essential, but not in the upper region of the organization chart. For many, their status changed and they joined the ranks of wives, but still retained their helping status. For the women who were already married, the necessities of secrecy and absorption in work created a communication gap and a separation between wives and husbands.

The habits of the wives who came from small nearby communities, and whose husbands were mechanical and construction workers, were very different from the wives of the men involved in research. The former were greater in number and had many skills that the other women did not have. They were more independent in the sense of possessing resourcefulness in meeting the demands of a new situation. They knew how to do all kinds of things—make a garden, can vegetables and so forth. The women who had lived on farms, especially, were accustomed to working physically and had capabilities which a lot of the wives of the scientists had to learn, and which they did not respect at first. These wives felt that some of the things that the rural women knew about and did were demeaning and that they were being deprived of many opportunities. The conflicts were much greater than you would find in a more normal, open community.

Then the two groups of women began to respect and appreciate each other. The country women, let's say, were always surprised that the other women were human. So they exchanged prejudices. For a while the two groups idealized each other, which was as unrealistic with them as in the same situation with the men. Eventually, the women reached the same accord. But many women had turned to each other for emotional intimacy and had learned a great deal from each other from which husbands found themselves excluded.

But with this much more realistic understanding of each other came a lot of clashing, and cliques began to form—the kind of thing you find in families. So that, both within the circles of the wives of professionals and the wives of others, there was a restatement of family relationships, of siblings, of others. Within these groups, they were essentially extended families. So the emotional intensity between them was much greater than you would find in a more-normal, less-closed community.

Letter XII

Oak Ridge, Tenn.
August 5, 1946

Dear Margaret,

We leave in two days for six weeks to investigate the outside world. Besides trying to figure how to cram everything into only five suitcases, getting the house ready for the painters, cleaning out the pretzels, potato chips and assorted crackers from the car, arranging last-minute instructions for our new occupant, proctoring one of Dick's students for an exam, there isn't a thing to do.

I had to get special permission from USED[1] to have the living room painted white. So far Irene has had three different colors of paint on her little bottom, and I am sure if we were to be here for the interior painting, she would look like an Indian on the warpath.

Thanks loads for the book.[2] When you were telling me about it, it sounded formidable. However, it is very readable and of great interest to me.

Oak Ridge is soon to boast of a country club—primarily for golfers. It will be limited to 500 members at $120 per, and it will be "first come, first served." Anybody is eligible, but the fee may prohibit many people. The fee is a membership fee, and there is a yearly fee of $50 plus $20 for associate members.

We had a lot of excitement with the elections here. Two days before the voting, an injunction was served to prevent us from voting. The powers that

---

[1]U.S. Engineer Department.

[2]*Yankee City.*

be in Tennessee consider Oak Ridge a menace. We got our vote, and now expect it to be contested.

All the buses have new signs prominently displayed: "Colored fares will ride in seats in the rear of the bus."

The girl who is taking over our house says she plans to have several friends spend a week with her, as a change from dorm life, and is inviting all the bachelors over for some decent food. Some of our friends have arranged with her to come over and play sonatas and listen to our records.

We expect to reach New York about August 20 and will be there until the middle of September. Will you be home by then? I shall try to call you at work. If you wish to reach us, we will be at 200 West 108th Street, Apartment 10C, New York City, Riv 9-2837.

Hope you, Gregory and Cathy are enjoying your summer.

Regards from Dick and

[sig] Thelma

Here are some remembrances I jotted down in 1980 of that summer in New York:

After the war, the annual meetings of the American Physical Society provided happy hunting grounds for reunions with friends who were scattered all over the country. Sylvia Reines and her husband[3] came all the way from Los Alamos to New York for the 1946 meeting, where she and I had a jolly time comparing notes on our sister cities. Although I have never been to Los Alamos, I learned that many of our experiences could have been applied there.

The afternoon before she was to leave, she told me of one plight she experienced in New York and how it was solved. She had spent the morning in Macy's and wound up in the gourmet department, lingering longingly at the display of all the tempting and mouth-watering items. Hardly any were available in New Mexico. She was practically drooling over one particularly splendid display. A clerk asked, "May I help you?"

She answered sadly, "I'm afraid you can't."

"What's your problem, madam?"

"Well," she replied, "you see, I live in Los Alamos, and I love New York bagels. But we're leaving tomorrow morning, and if I buy some now, they'll be hard as rocks by the time we get home."

He asked her if she was flying and if she owned a freezer, and she said "yes" to both questions.

"Well then, we can help you. You know, Macy's has a special service for

---

[3]Dr. Fred Reines is a distinguished, prominent physicist and had been one of my husband's graduate students at New York University.

customers like you. All you have to do is place your order and pay for it, and you will be given a number. Our drive-in booth is open twenty-four hours a day. On your way to the airport, just stop by—you don't even have to get out of your taxi—show your number to the window clerk and you will be handed your frozen bagels packed in dry ice. You can pop them in your freezer as soon as you get home." (I believe their slogan was something like "99% satisfied customers.")

And I think Sylvia bought enough bagels to last her family until our next annual reunion!

Letter XIII

Oak Ridge, Tenn.
Sept. 30, 1946

Dear Margaret,

Our parole was up, so here we are behind the bars again. I had hoped very much to see you when we were in New York, and called your home to find out that you were not expected back until the fifteenth. There were so many things I wanted to talk over with you, but we were due back here on the fourteenth.

We had a fine trip, and after driving 3,000 miles, Oak Ridge still seems like another world. Outside the billboards display polar bears sitting on ice cubes drinking Pepsi-Cola, magnificent cars driving up the highest mountains with Esso. Here they show wise old owls telling you to keep your mouth shut, or Uncle Sam pointing at you to BE CAREFUL. Instead of little signs nailed on a tree saying "Private Property—Keep Off," here they say "Restricted area—no one permitted without permit."

There have been many changes. The hospital is now called Medical Arts Building—all doctors now have private practices (all their offices are still in the hospital). The telephone system has been turned over to Southern Bell Telephone Company. All of the housing maintenance is under a new management, but the Army still makes decisions as to who shall have what. We have a new department store (a concession, of course), and they, in turn, have several concessions within the store. All of the boardwalks are being removed on the main streets and are being replaced with gravel walks and a rather primitive type of drainage system. Interest in the Town Council has been revived, and elections are next week.

There will be a councilman for each of the nine districts, as well as three councilmen-at-large. One interesting feature is that a Negro is running from

113

his district, AND it has been agreed that the future councilmen will sit around the same table with him—if he is elected. At a committee meeting of the League of Women Voters, we decided to hold a candidates' meeting next week; and quite a discussion followed whether or not we should send a formal invitation to the Negroes on the area. There was also some doubt about roping off a section for any who might show up, and it was considered unnecessary since we felt that they would sit in the rear of the auditorium of their own accord.

Maid service has been taken over entirely by Community Relations. In order to get a badge, each maid must have a Wasserman. The badge is good for ninety days, after which another test is required, etc. Also, each housewife is requested to indicate by postal card how she rates any new maid. In this way, the woman in charge (who told me all this) hopes to weed out the poor quality workers. She said there are so many who want to come here to work that she can afford to be choosy.

Enclosed is a leaflet for Oak Ridge teachers. From all reports I have heard, the schools here are supposed to be very, very good. Certainly a great deal of attention is focused upon the welfare of the children. There is an excellent bus system for the schools, and the children are even brought home for lunch. There are over 7,000 enrolled in all the schools here, with 709 in high school, 1387 in junior high, and the rest in grade schools and kindergarten. The Negro school has 43 students.

Oak Ridge is just bursting with activity now that summer is over. All the clubs are having elections, fall programs are being announced, and it is a busy city indeed.

As for me, I think I may now claim to be a typical Oak Ridge housewife—my last resistance has been broken. Company expected, bakeries closed, what to do! So I baked my first batch of cookies. Alas, they were delicious and now I am doomed. My special system to keep them from burning is to play one movement of a Mozart sonata while they are baking, put in another batch and play another movement, etc.

I have about finished the book you sent me. Dick picked up Ruth Benedict's "Patterns of Culture," and we have fun exchanging our reading experiences. I am looking forward to reading the rest of the volumes in the Yankee City Series. Dick is going to see if they are in the University of Tennessee library, which would eliminate the nuisance of mailing.

One of the reasons I wanted to see you was to find out whether you are interested in the things I write you. You might be interested in certain aspects of living here thåt I haven't touched on. Suggestions or criticism will be cheerfully accepted.

Dick liked Gregory's article[1] in the Bulletin.

We both hope you had a nice summer and are feeling fine.

As ever,
[sig] Thelma

---

[1] Gregory Bateson, "Pattern of an Armaments Race," *Bulletin of Atomic Scientists*, vol. 2, Sept. 1, 1946, nos. 5 and 6, p. 10, 11, Part I.

October 1946
72 Perry Street
New York City

Dear Thelma,

Yes, that is what I was afraid would happen. We couldn't get back before the fifteenth. It was so wasteful to miss you. But I am enjoying the things you write about so much. I was interested in the clipping—or rather flier—for Oak Ridge teachers. No mention of the community differing from any other. It might be interesting to list the areas where it is articulately admitted that the community is different, or was different and isn't, or isn't anything but a Tennessee town, or perhaps a Tennessee town with an invasion of Northerners. You might watch for that. I see that the CIO must have quieted down. What's happening now?

Now about this oft-bruited subject of our making a flying trip down to see you. Is it still an open possibility, or have you now a houseful of permanent guests—as most people have these days? And how long does it take to get there? Gregory lectures till 8 on Friday nights, which means our weekends are just two days. If we could get there overnight some Friday and return on Sunday night, we might at least get the feel of things. Or perhaps we could fly—especially if there is a night plane. I would be a great deal more use if I could really see your setting once.

Myself, I've been through the throes of moving from New Hampshire, painting, a family of five, because I now have an 18-year-old daughter of a friend of mine who is going to Barnard, and I also had the 8-year-old daughter of a friend who is in the hospital. We still have no rugs down or curtains up, but life is getting a little neater and a little cleaner each day.

Gregory sends his regards.

Yours,
[sig] Margaret

Letter XIV

Dear Margaret,

After all the publicity and buildup for the election of members of our Town Council, our candidates meeting was some flop—there being almost more candidates than audience. Our only consolation was the fact that we were competing that same night with a football game and a "Turtle Derby" sponsored by the Lions Club. In making their bid for our vote, however, several candidates spoke of Oak Ridge as a "city of significance" and a "city with a purpose—even since the war is over," or a desire to help "build" a "model city" and a special emphasis on the transition period from Army to civilian control.

The results of the elections proved rather conclusively that we have an embryo political machine starting here. The clique that wanted to get in did some heavy electioneering and brought carloads of people (particularly young, irresponsible people from the dorms) to the voting places, and they did get in. This is all adding to the confusion here about the future status of Oak Ridge. I hope to be able to give you details when we see you.

Some of the questions that have arisen are how far can we go towards being a "normal" city under the McMahon Bill,[1] what type of municipal government can we have, must we conform to the laws of the state of Tennessee, as

---

[1]The McMahon Act took control of the country's atomic program from the Army and gave it to a civilian commission. The act was signed August 1, 1946, and became effective the following January 1, though the commission did not take office until April. The legislation was named for Senator Brian McMahon of Connecticut, chairman of the Senate-House Joint Atomic Energy Committee.

117

long as we have power plants here under the A.D.A. (if it goes through), must we be a gated area, and can a gated area become an incorporated community? I tell you many civic groups and individuals are just dizzy trying to figure these things out.

Take teachers, for instance. The average salary here is about $2,300. They are paid by the county with a special fund allotted just to them from the Government. One of the main attractions in Oak Ridge is the fact that the schools are so good. The enclosed pamphlet will give you an idea how we tower over the rest of the state in education.

Residents here are by no means unanimous in wanting civilian control. Your home is maintained at no extra expense, coal is brought to your bin every Wednesday, you don't have to decide when you want your house painted—it's done for you, electricity is free, no property taxes. Further, there are plenty who feel that the "gates" protect us from the "outside."

But, more and more, people are beginning to feel that Oak Ridge is "home." They are interested in settling here and watching it grow. This, in spite of such common expressions as "Oak Ridge Jitters" or "Oak Ridgitis."

There is a lot of social climbing here of a most peculiar sort. If one gets an invitation to a fashion show sponsored by Army Wives, that's going up. Quite a study could be made on the "things" and "people" that matter. Anyway, the Army wives are "swank" here. We, poor souls, belong in "lower snob nob." Then, too, this being a "company town," chiefs of personnel are VERY important.

Women are beginning to be less embarrassed about being clothes-conscious. Hats and gloves are à la mode. Even our department store has its exclusive Town and Country Shop with simple, little classic numbers for only $79.95. One hears more women talking about luncheon appointments and a great yearning for a Schrafftsy tearoom.

Perhaps it is an effort to break away from the same pattern of living that most people have here. Everybody knows that almost the whole town rises at the same time. Now that the weather is cooler, you begin to see smoke coming from all the chimneys each morning. You see groups of men and women waiting at the bus stops for special buses that take them to the "lab" or "plant," and you know that about 5 o'clock they'll all be hopping off the bus— the working day over. If you walk up any street about 5:30 P.M. and peek at all the kitchens, all the wives are preparing supper; and later, if you pass again you see plenty of husbands scowling over the dishes.

Once a month the movie calendar comes out, which tells you what is playing and when in the five theaters here. You see them in all the homes, and then all the sitters are notified what nights to save.

When a scarce item is on hand in your neighborhood market, neighbors pass the word around. You drop everything, no matter what, and dash over before it is all gone.

So long,
[sig] Thelma

Bettie Levy also commented on the change in dress, saying that the informality lasted until houses started going to private ownership a good many years after the town developed. In her words:

> The ladies started putting on their gloves and their high heels. That was the reaction when some went all-out to wear New York fashions. I am a very informal type and just loved it when you didn't have to dress up to go out and everybody wore casual clothes. When a department store came to Oak Ridge, it meant a great deal to many, but it also varied in other cases. The nice thing about Oak Ridge is that you can have this tremendous gamut going from formal to very informal and doing your own thing, which is now what everybody does here in the '80s. But to do it in the '50s was pretty avant-garde.
>
> This is one of the things that makes living here so pleasant.

Julia Moore, who had been teaching school in Middle Tennessee, recalled her reasons for coming to Oak Ridge, her arrival, and the schools she found there in her 1980 panel speech:

> Well, I think this is supposed to be called "Pioneering in the Oak Ridge Schools." It was pioneering because it was a brand new school system. It had been established within the year before I came here, in August of 1944.
>
> I came because I had written three friends with whom I had lost contact, and I wondered where in the world they were. I found out that all of them were some place nobody knew where, and I got letters from them saying, "Oh, come, come. It's great! We have a good salary of $210 a month for ten months."
>
> During the summer of 1944, I got on the bus and came to Oak Ridge. There was a pass waiting for me at the gate. I came in and finally found myself at the dormitory, W-5, where my friend was.
>
> During the few days I was here, I had a conference with Dr. [A. H.]Blankenship, and before I even got home from Oak Ridge, my county superintendent at home had heard from him asking to write a recommendation, clearance and everything like that. That is how I happened to come here. I guess the $210 just pulled me right in. They also told me that we had unlimited freedom in our teaching. There were kindergartens, music teachers, art teachers, gym teachers, and a library in the schools. That was something I never had in a county school in Maury County or in Rutherford County. I just thought I was entering into the land of milk and honey as far as school was concerned.
>
> Eventually, time came for me to pack my car, which I did, putting in my rocking chair that Santa Claus had given me several years before, to take to school. I had a few flowers, a box of old school supplies, thumbtacks, paperclips, and things I would need on my desk. The last thing I bought that morning before I left Columbia was a red raincoat, and that was about the first

thing I needed when I got to Oak Ridge. Because we did have rain and red, red mud.

School was just what it was put up to be—unlimited possibilities to do anything we wanted at school. However, the school building we went into, Glenwood, was not quite complete. The building, I guess, was complete, but the furniture was not there. So we did our first few days sitting on the floor and teaching maybe from a blackboard, maybe we had some chalk. They were called chalkboards then and were green, and we had yellow chalk. We did our teaching that way for a while.

Eventually we got furniture, but in the classrooms for the second-graders, some of the tables were entirely too high. I asked the custodian if he would saw off the legs. No'm, he couldn't do that—he didn't belong to the carpenter's union and they'd get him if he did that.

I said, "Would you please get me a saw and I'll do it!"

He got me a saw and I sawed off the legs. I put all of them into my toy box or block box. Why I kept this one all this long, I do not know. Anyway, here is the evidence that I sawed off the table legs, and I did not belong to a union, so I could get by with that.

Along with our school duties, we eventually had a double-shift program. People were still coming in streams, still with oodles of children, and the flattops out around Glenwood were filling up. I guess they rented them out to boarders; I know some of them did. Teaching double-shift meant that I went to school at 8A.M. and taught till 12 and cleared out at 12:30. Another teacher came in with another group and taught from 12:30 until 4:30. That was the program for about a year or more. It was odd being chased out of your room for half a day, but we got used to it and did our planning in other parts of the school.

We had Saturday workshops. In fact, we were greeted with workshops when we first came to Oak Ridge. We were briefed one way or the other about everything that was going to happen in those days. We had maybe a speaker sometimes; but eventually, the workshops were a good way for us to meet each other and get new ideas from each other.

During the first two years, everybody in the school system worked on a great big, thick book—I think it weighed fifteen pounds. It was called "A Guide to Teaching in Oak Ridge Schools." That was rewritten and revised, and the second "Guide to Teaching"—fully as thick—was written. We put in many long hours. That was part of our "in-service training," only the term had not been coined then. The Oak Ridge schools were a showplace from the beginning, because the purse strings were loose and we had so many advantages that schools in surrounding counties did not have. They would send teachers and superintendents over to see us. You never knew when there would be people walking into your room quietly observing what you were doing and what you were teaching. Maybe there would be a little panel afterwards and maybe not. But we were host to many, many visitors for a number of years.

After the A-bomb had been dropped (we all felt so patriotic!), they gave out pins to those who were still living here. Those who were here the longest got a silver pin. Others got a little bronze pin. Here is my A pin showing that I lived and worked here during the war years.

Lydia Bredig had worked six years as a psychologist at Bellevue Hospital and one year at the Child Guidance Institute in New York and in two private schools in Manhattan. She came to Oak Ridge with her husband, Max, a chemist from the Vanadium Corporation in New York, who welcomed the chance to do fundamental research. Lydia continues:

> For us, the decision to leave New York was made in deference to my husband's professional needs. I was happy for a new experience, but we kept some books and the apartment in New York—just in case. A visit to Oak Ridge made the decision about where we were going. I was told that the people at the labs were all you could hope for: intensely involved in their work, ideal research was being done, a congenial and alive community in a beautiful country. And assurances, of course, that "your wife will find work in her profession."
>
> So we piled into a Buick of questionable age and turned south. Eighty-five miles out, the Buick leaked water. We got acquainted with ponds, rivers and gas stations along the way. And we arrived the next day very late at night to a very dark gate. Well, there was a pass for Dr. Bredig. He was expected. No pass for his wife. We waited, listening to the silences of the night, playing with the fantasies of an armed camp, until someone arrived with cheeriness, apologies and good humor. The next few days I rocked on the porch of the then Guest House, watching people come and go—mostly go on—while the conviction settled in me that I was an appendage and was allotted so much room but not much more. Rocking in the sunshine lost its charm after a few days.
>
> A call to a psychiatrist in town to inquire about work opportunities deepened my shock. He and his colleague were very friendly and confidential. They were leaving, primarily, beacuse they felt that the people who took over after the war—particularly the doctors, who were Army-oriented, were assuming authority, dominance and direction of how work should be done, and were very autocratic. Now that the war was over, these two men felt that they would have more freedom and more opportunity to work elsewhere, which turned out to be true. They felt that the Army kind of direction, which the community took, developed a point of view where some professionals assumed that they were the political leaders of the community in a way that they could not have in an open community, and that their personal prejudices took precedence over professional concerns. These two men were professional people who had been here under the Army, and they were leaving because they were particularly concerned about the medical profession.
>
> They told me, "This is what you learn. You are facing a professional bias against your profession."
>
> At that time, it didn't sink in. But it was the first inkling of a kind of community where values were different, but not too different.

The two psychiatrists wished me luck and went their way—to international eminence and esteem in their profession. During the next few weeks while we waited for housing, in what was the former barracks at Jefferson Circle, there were evoked and acted out the traumas of my life. I finally conceded that I didn't need a maid twice a week to clean the venetian blinds—the Elevated of Third Avenue and the soot of New York were far away. I could turn off the electricity in the oven another way than pulling the whole unit out and needing help in putting it back. There was an established community ready to extend welcome, offering vacuum cleaners, lunch, parties and friendship. But I needed to get up and be done with dismay and join the exuberance and vitality surrounding me.

As a way of getting acquainted in Oak Ridge and having an excuse, other than breaking a tooth, to get to New York, I did a study of two groups of third- and fourth-grade children in Oak Ridge schools. One was of the children from families predominantly in helping-situations at work, and one was of children from families whose fathers were employed as scientists and in the technical field. Even though the houses were assigned according to family size, by 1946 there were neighborhoods where the organizational chart was a factor of choice.

The findings concerning these two groups, compared to a group in New York from families of moderate incomes to really affluent parents, gave surprising results. There was a significant difference in the pattern of psychological development of the two Oak Ridge groups—those whose parents came from predominantly rural areas (Group A) compared to Group B, whose parents tended to be in scientific and administrative fields. The pattern of Group B was very similar to Group C, the New York group. Those in Group A seemed to have missed their latency period of development and were behaving more like preadolescents and adolescents.

It was not that they were necessarily mature, as it later turned out, but they were more practical, had developed a sense of themselves, and the confidence that they could take care of themselves and be physically more aggressive and playful. Because of their sheer numbers, self-certainty, and aggressiveness, these children were very influential in establishing their value systems, and others tended to look toward them for leadership. They became the dominant group and set the style of what was IN and what was OUT.

Letter XV

Oak Ridge, Tenn.
Oct. 26, 1946

Dear Margaret,

The party season is on in Oak Ridge, and last week activities reached a new high—particularly for the Clinton Labbers. There were over 100 visiting scientists here for an "information meeting." In addition to dinner parties, a smoker for men only, three "D" houses had open house one night for all the visitors, scientific staff and wives. During the course of the evening we were all expected to visit each of the three houses. The "D" houses are next to the biggest ones here, and the living rooms can easily hold about a hundred people—standing.

We have had many of these parties. Almost any pretext is used to give one. And they all follow a similar pattern. Because residents know the type of houses, everyone knows where to hang their coats, where the bathroom is, and where to go for a drink of water. Before things really warm up, people stand around in clusters. There is always a variety of drinks (despite this being a dry county). Then a small group of old-timers get off in a corner and start singing. We have heard the same songs sung at every party, and they are sung year after year. After a while you get to know them and find yourself joining in and liking it.

People get to know each other pretty well, that is, within their own social strata, but intimate friendships are rare. There is something about this place that lets us go so far, but never completely let our "hair down." I think this is particularly difficult on women. Lately I have been hearing a lot of talk from women either having psychiatric treatment or feeling the need of it.

The Good Government Group of the League of Women Voters has an interesting program this year, and I have heard some enlightening talks. We are investigating the social and welfare agencies in the area. I have talked with the head of the Red Cross and Juvenile Department. Next week I am looking forward to a meeting with the head of the Medical Social Service.

The Red Cross is in an exceptional position here. Originally, they were asked to come here by the Government in anticipation of more than the usual amount of problems expected. They were asked to extend their services beyond their usual activities and to handle all welfare cases because of their record of efficiency in operation. They were, and still are, the only agency here with funds at their disposal. I may have mentioned that 93 percent of the money raised in their annual drive is retained here.

Most of the money is spent for medical attention and funeral bills. (We have no funeral homes here and funerals are handled by nearby cities.) They discovered many cases of truancy among young girls due to lack of proper clothing. Then there was the period when overtime pay—which kept most families going—stopped, and the families were not prepared for the decrease in income. Then there were problems due to the tremendous younger girl and older man population, tragic accidents in the early part of the project, insufficient provision for rehabilitating new workers recruited, the need for loans, the need for Christmas baskets and toys. Last December a survey disclosed that 187 children would have been without a decent Christmas, and baskets were given to forty families. Incidentally, the firemen collected old toys, fixed them up, and the "grey" ladies painted dolls' faces and made dresses for them. They still have an average caseload of 240 a month, with a limited and less-trained staff than other agencies here, and now feel that since there are competent groups in existence, they should be relieved of some of the burden and let the other agencies have the freedom to develop as they should.

As it is, the other agencies must make their referrals to the Red Cross for financial aid. The "powers that be," commonly called "the Hill" or District Engineers, have rejected a request for a Community Chest, and apparently don't see the need for any change in policy. They may have some justification in their reasons. They feel that a drive would not be very successful because there is, as yet, no community awareness or civic feeling. The people don't get behind things (including the P-TA). A majority of families feel insecure due to the terminations at some of the plants.

According to the head of the Juvenile Department, who is also coordinator for all agencies here, the position of the Red Cross hampers their work. Some of the prevalent juvenile cases are vandalism, truancy, petty larceny and some sex delinquency in adolescent girls. They have thirty-five to forty cases a month, and what surprised me is his claim that while cases come from all parts of the area, there seems to be more in Townsite and from permanent homes sections. On the whole, from his experience, the amount of cases are about like any average communty. The trailer section seems to be settling down as the red light district. And, incidentally, many trailer families have been offered permanent homes and have turned them down due to the low wage scale.

One of the problems besetting the agencies is peculiar to Oak Ridge. It is a question of residency. Oak Ridgers don't accrue legal residency in Tennessee, and after remaining here for a period, many of them lose their rights of residency from their former states. In case of death of the family wage-earner or of termination, the family must leave.

One of the branches of the Oak Ridge Welfare Service is the Nesper House, which recently opened for emergency care of children. There was a particular need for it here, because so few families have relatives to rely on in case of emergency. I understand that a colored child was admitted, without hesitation, but it was kept quiet from the community. The heads are hoping it won't become an open question, as it is a ticklish question here.

Every day one of the markets gets in a "scarce item." One day it seemed as if we had an epidemic of diarrhea. Every other housewife was running home with a roll of toilet tissue. My neighbor called me from her office to get her some. I met another neighbor in the store with her babe in arm, and she whispered that the child had "loaded" pants and she didn't want to take time to change her.

We had an open meeting of our League of Women Voters last week and were delighted to see about ten members of the YCAC.[1] They are a bunch of enthusiastic kids and very articulate. I asked one of them about their magazine and was told it was suspended over the summer. They are hoping to start it again. At present they are devoting themselves to speaking tours, and writing editorials for magazines, including McCall's, Woman's Home Companion, Seventeen, etc. They meet twice a week and usually have a scientist talk to them. They are anxious to get adults to attend their meeting so they can "influence their votes." They had 250 members at their peak. A lot of their members left the area, and some have quit because they are jealous and resentful when they are not asked to speak or write. But one girl said very seriously, "That's our fault. We have failed to make everyone see that they have an important job, and we must correct it." I shall certainly try to attend some of their meetings.

By the way, I hope I made it clear that any weekend would be fine for you to come. Right now, the autumn coloring is at its height and is very beautiful. I almost hate to have you miss it.

Dick has been busier than usual. He was invited to give some lectures at the new training school, otherwise known as "superman's school." He is also going in for freehand drawing. From 7:30 to 8 P.M. he makes piggies, doggies and horsies for Irene, and by golly, she recognizes them!

I hope you get the package of clippings, etc. The information booklet was given to every resident and is quite useful to us and especially to newcomers. There has been such a demand for extra copies, an extra edition has been put out for sale for a nominal sum.

And so to bed. With regards to all.

[sig] Thelma

---

[1]Youth Council on the Atomic Crisis.

Rose and Cy Feldman differed with me about Oak Ridge ties and friendships and felt they were more a part of the community than they would have been in a big city. Here's what Rose had to say in her interview:

> We lived in a flattop for almost three years until 1949. When we were expecting Alice, we applied for a cemesto house. Cy was a civilian by then—he had been discharged from the Army in 1946.
>
> It's funny, a lot our friends were pressuring us to move into a cemesto. But we really loved that little house and the neighborhood. We didn't have a car, and there was a bus stop at the end of our street that went to the end of the line. We've sort of kept in touch with some of the people who were there. There was a bond with friends we made. We were all away from home and had no families here. The friends we made were really our families. We had only a little bit of contact with people outside of Oak Ridge. If you didn't have a car, you were limited. At the time we came, the average age among the scientists was 27, so almost the whole community was the same age, and you could really pick compatible people instantly. We put down roots very quickly here.
>
> We lived in the C house almost four years, during which time our fourth child was born. The night before Robbie (our fifth) was born, we were finally assigned a D house. We took the first one they offered us, because we were really falling all over each other. We went to fix up the house that evening—they didn't clean houses in those days. It had been occupied by six single young men and was painted gray on the inside. I cleaned out the linen and kitchen closets and put paper down. Some of my neighbors helped me move my kitchen supplies. I was appalled at the amount of Jello I had on hand. I scrubbed and cleaned until about 11:30 P.M. and went home. Robbie was born at 4:30 the next morning, just barely after I got to the hospital. Daddy finished the moving.

New York City
Oct. 31, 1946

Dear Thelma,

This is just a hasty note to say that I don't think we will be able to get down until after Christmas. Your second unanswered long letter came this morning. I wish we could come sooner, but I just don't see how to do it.

Sincerely,
[*sig*] Margaret

As I wrote Margaret, I found that people tended to keep to themselves and their own kind and that intimate friendships outside of one's milieu were rare. But in the early days of Oak Ridge, such was clearly not the case for Rose Feldman, and also particularly not for Ruth Carey who, in her interview, enlarged on Rose's remarks that friends were family:

> Milton had been with the TVA in Knoxville. He started working in Oak Ridge in 1943, and we moved out here with our six-year-old child about the

first of the next year. I was only twenty-two at the time. Before we came to Oak Ridge, Milton would come out by bus or a car would come by the house to pick him up. Things were so urgent that they wanted to make sure people could get here, even though the roads were really terrible. He had a very secret job at the time, testing various components they were using in the gaseous diffusion process of trying to split the atom.

When we first moved here, we didn't know anybody except a couple of young men who were in the Army. When it came time for us to move, the Army sent a big flatbed truck for our things. We put our possessions, such as they were, on it, and the three of us got on the truck with our stuff. I remember standing on that flatbed all the way out here. When we got here, two young men who were in the Army came over to help us. People were tremendously helpful and compatible, especially the young men in the Army. They were lonely, and they liked the idea of being with a family, and we were all young and had a nice time together. Some of the ones we met at that time had been picked for their science and engineering backgrounds and they turned out to be tremendously interesting people. Some are still our friends.

We had never been very religiously inclined, but to make social contacts, we went to a Jewish congregation which met, like the other denominations, in the Chapel on the Hill. We met a lot of people that way. There was a fairly large Jewish group here, and that was an interesting aspect of those early days. The reason was that so many young Jewish men went into the sciences and mathematics and engineering, and these were the fields that they needed so badly here that they were taken out of Army camps and brought to Oak Ridge.

I didn't find the change difficult because I didn't come out of a place where I had a beautiful home or something. We had lived very simply up to that time; we were just out of the Depression. Any place we could get, we just had a great time. Living in a little flattop was an adventure, and we had it full of people all the time. As a matter of fact, we actually wore it out with all those shoes tromping through the house.

When we first came shifts were around the clock, and Milton was working from 3 until 11 the first couple of months. That removed him from the social scene completely. So I took my child and we went around and made our own friends. We would get to know one person, and through that one we would meet another person. They had recreational things, like the dances on the tennis courts, and we met people through the Jewish congregation. We just met people through each other.

(Were they mostly scientists, though, at that level?—*T.P.*)

Yes, I guess they really were, though they were in the Army. We just mixed with anybody we came in contact with. But I found that because you didn't talk about your work and you didn't identify yourself with your work, that it was a completely democratic social interaction between people. You made friends. I don't like to use the word "accepted," but you were accepted by other people as a friend just through your own personality. You didn't have to prove that you were successful in science or in some other field to make these friends. We would get together through concerts or anything that was of a common interest and not through situations where you had stratas of society.

(This was what interested me, because when we came here it definitely was stratified, because by that time in 1946 things had sort of settled down. We only knew other scientists and had no contact with any other part of town. I am curious to know what sort of interaction there was in the early days.—*T.P.*)

The experience for me was very broad as far as social contacts were concerned, because I made social contacts in the Jewish congregation, I made social contacts in my interest in music and then art, and then in the business community. You'd go to a store, or through a child from school—just any sort of situation that you found yourself in—and you made all sorts of contacts.

We weren't concerned about what somebody's work was, and later on when the secrecy was no longer present I was always being surprised to find out that a guy was very prominent in some field. It just never occurred to me to be curious about it, because I knew better than to ask questions. The first time it came home to me personally about the degree of not asking questions was in the Central Cafeteria, which was a great gathering place. I was sitting there once with a group and several other people joined us. They knew the other people there and one of the people was Jack _____. It turned out later that he was one of the co-discoverers of promethium[2], but to me he was just another one of the people who were sitting there. I said, "Where do you work?" meaning in what location, I didn't want to ask him about his work, but he just turned his head and I thought, "Oh, my God, I have asked him a question that I shouldn't have." But I wasn't disturbed about it and I just changed the subject.

(But you did find life here distinctly different?—*T.P.*)

Oh, yes, it was completely different. It wasn't a shock, it was an adventure. As I told you, my husband was out of the social picture altogether for the first few months because of the hours he worked. When he came off that shift and had some evenings free, he said, "Well, let me meet some of the friends you already know," and then he got in the picture and we had a terrific time. It was really a good time in our life, we made friendships then that we have retained until this day, that are so close that they are more like family. People were very interested in each other's children, and the children became sort of community property.

---

[2]A metallic element of the rare-earth group obtained as a fission product of uranium.

(I think that generally, because of the Oak Ridge setup, friendships were probably much closer and had much more meaning here than in any other city.—*T.P.*)

Oh, they did. You became extended families. It all depended on your own acceptance of other people without question. Your relationships were formed on your own interest in each other as people, and not as a status-seeker. To me, that was not part of the picture at all. I think that it affected our ability to enjoy people all the rest of our lives, and not to look at it from the standpoint that they're helping you climb a social ladder.

(Were you aware of any resentment toward the scientists, since they were sort of the elite in Oak Ridge?—*T.P.*)

I didn't have any personally. My husband was not a prominent scientist, not in the context Waldo [Cohn] was, or some of the other people we met. We met them and became very friendly with them and retained our friendships to this day. You had the opportunity to enjoy friendships with people from tremendously diverse backgrounds, from very different kinds of places, just on a completely personal basis.

Irene and me playing with "Thurber" under the porch of our house. Courtesy the author

Richard and Irene on the boardwalk that led from the back of our house to a nearby shopping area. Courtesy the author

Rose Feldman and her first child Joan in front of their "victory cottage." Courtesy Rose Feldman

A few families who worked for the L&N Railroad lived in special units like this one converted from a boxcar. Everette A. Hale stands on the porch of his home, which consisted of a living room, two bedrooms, and kitchen. Such units had no running water or toilet facilities. Courtesy Shirley H. Brooks

Most senior scientists, top-ranking army personnel, and executive level civilians lived in single-unit family cemesto houses. Constructed of cement-asbestos material, units were designated "A" through "H", according to floor plan and size. Moving into Oak Ridge with one child, we were assigned this two bedroom "B" house on Delaware Avenue. Courtesy the author

One of the challenges of living in a "B" house was coping with a different stove. My first great accomplishment was a successful pie. Photo by Ed Wescott. Courtesy Department of Energy.

Residents of the dormitories lived in rooms furnished with the barest of necessities. Photo by Ed Wescott. Courtesy Department of Energy

Letter XVI

Oak Ridge, Tenn.
Nov. 24, 1946

Dear Margaret,

We were so sorry to hear that you have to put off your visit with us, as we had been looking forward to it. There is a possibility of our coming to New York for the Christmas holidays, if Dick has a long enough vacation.

I have been extremely busy this past month. There have been many meetings to attend, several investigations for the League of Women Voters, more than the usual social engagements and just to complicate life a little more, I have started piano lessons again. The latter means going into Knoxville once a week.

The Town Council had its first open meeting since the election, and the attendance of about 300 was considered excellent. Many people aired their "gripes." Most of the complaints came from dormitory dwellers—their lack of facilities, no privacy, having to eat all meals in restaurants (with poor quality food, high prices, small portions, unattractive and dirty). There were complaints against the telephone company for starting to charge tolls on calls to Knoxville and surrounding towns. It is also a nuisance to call anyone at the plants now. They have their own operators controlled by the Army, and it is necessary to dial a special operator first and give your number. Apparently there are not enough lines, because they are always busy and we usually have to call several times. Incidentally, all of the members of the council were introduced to the audience as Mr. So-and-So, etc., but when the Negro was introduced, he was called Wadkins. I think most of the people were curious to know how much power the Council will have and how it will be affected when the Commission takes over.

135

Everyone is talking about the Commission, and many groups and organizations are busy drawing up recommendations to them.

The people seem more unsettled than ever and are anxious to know what will be the status of Oak Ridge. At first, many were glad that the gates might be taken away, but now they are not so sure. Time and again one hears that the gates offer us a lot of protection. Most people would like a voice as to how the town should be run. They would like an uncensored paper, and all the advantages of a normal town. On the other hand, if the gates are taken away, they will have to lock their doors, they will lose the convenience of house maintenance, there will be all kinds of soliciting permitted, there will be no "control" over the people allowed to come here to live and there will be "free enterprise."

One of the biggest problems is the schools. According to a talk with the superintendent of schools, the greatest factor in keeping the population here is the standard of education. But if adequate housing for teachers is not made available, the teachers will leave. The teachers here also feel they have no status in the community, that they are not "accepted." He feels it would be "fatal" if the schools were turned back to the state. Some other points he brought out were the unusual amounts of fluctuation and turnover here, this being an abnormal place as far as age distribution—the largest age group is the 1-year-olds, which will mean a kindergarten problem in four years. Tennessee schools have no kindergartens.

Enclosed is a sketchy outline of a report made to the League of Women Voters and our News Letter. The latter will give you an idea of the scope of our activities.

I had some quite interesting visits to the colored Hutments. We spoke to the head of the colored school. This has just been started, and there are about sixty children enrolled. There are two teachers, and they have their hands full. Most of the children never attended school at all, and the biggest problem is getting them adjusted socially. They haven't been able to get all of the children to come to school, and it is almost impossible to check on those who do not attend. The age groups in the classrooms are at variance. There is no eighth grade (no students qualified for it), but a few have requested to go to high school.

For those wishing high school, provisions are made to send them to Knoxville by bus. Expenses will be paid from the school budget here. There is, as yet, no provision for preschool children. This makes it very difficult for working mothers. Up until now there have been no recreational facilities at all for children except a poolroom or the cafeteria. But there was an announcement this week that a recreation place is being started.

We also spoke to the Negro councilman, who is also the assistant public relations man at the Hutments. There are 702 of these—a few of them contain families and have an oil stove. None of them have running water. The rest of the families live in the 220 Victory Cottages. These have two rooms, bathroom and water. The total population is between 1600 and 1700. Of these, 1,000 are considered permanent residents. There are no regulations about people moving here, except that they must show a work badge when they pay rent.

But there are many that are unemployed (some by choice) who still manage to retain their badges; and many part-time workers.

The only work available here [for Negroes] is house work, common labor and janitoring. He feels that the character of the place is improving, and they are trying to investigate people moving here. They have their own colored council, and he feels that they have been able to do a great deal for the people. He is proud of the fact that they are able to get action much faster than the regular Town Council and are not bothered by the red tape. According to him, the people seem quite satisfied with their life in Oak Ridge and would be more so if they had more recreation facilities.

At social gatherings here, part of the evening is usually taken up with exchanges of anecdotes and experiences with these houses. The newcomers find it a constant source of amazement and annoyance. The old-timers listen with amused tolerance and retaliate with tales of the "old days." There is usually a lot of speculation as to why things are done in a certain way and how the new housing management will carry on. I have never been any place where people talk so much about the houses they live in.

And now it is time for Irene's nose drops and Dick's hot tea with lemon. So long for now,

[sig] Thelma

If the hutment area had minimal recreational facilities, there was no lack of them in other parts of Oak Ridge. Here's more of what Helen Jernigan said in 1980:

At Carbide, I worked on the plant newspaper, the *Carbide Courier*, and in the recreation department. Carbide had much recreation for its employees, including a Canter Club, for women, with horseback-riding lessons. Many people participated. They had softball, basketball, bowling, and there were aerial trips; you could take an airplane trip from the Municipal Airport [in Knoxville] and pay $8 and go to Chattanooga, Lookout Mountain, Muscle Shoals, Chickamauga, Wheeler and Wilson Dams, visit TVA and over the Smokies. They were available for any group of twenty-seven Carbide employees. (I don't know why twenty-seven; I suppose that was the capacity of the plane.)

A lot was going on in recreation, and single people found ways to participate in a great deal of it. Nobody exactly sat around by the fire.

Letter XVII

Oak Ridge, Tenn.
Dec. 10, 1946

Dear Margaret,

Just two days before you sent me "Small Town," I read a review of it and was on the verge of sending for a copy. You can imagine how delighted I was to receive it. I shall bring it back when we come to New York Christmas, along with "Yankee City." Did you notice that Hicks mentions Warner? It [Hicks] is one of the few books of its nature that I have read written from a subjective point of view. In some respects, this is an advantage, and for one thing may have more popular appeal. But I get the feeling sometimes that his personal ideas get in the way. However, I am enjoying it and many things "hit home."

Our "Survey of Oak Ridge" is going along at a great pace and has stimulated much interest among members of the League of Women Voters as well as key people and groups here. From reports of members who have had interviews, almost everyone was cordially received and got good cooperation. The man in charge of housing was somewhat reticent, but made a surprising admission.

As I once wrote you, the Army has overall charge of the houses, but each plant has an allotment. Strictly, the policy is to distribute houses to employees according to the size of the family with no discrimination. However, he stated that special concessions are made to keep and satisfy certain needed men, in spite of any ill feeling which might result.

The geographic distribution has changed a lot since the beginning of Oak Ridge. In the "old" part of town, it was not unusual to see a whole block of houses, or even a whole street, inhabited by employees of one company. As the city enlarged, the houses were more interspersed. This may be one of the reasons why newcomers have more difficulty making friends. The key men of

Monsanto live in a group of houses close to each other in a choice section. They are a close social unit. They also have oil heaters—the plutocrats.

I had been under the impression that the Town Council was in a position to try to bring about small changes that the people request. But I find that they may only [do so] in an advisory way. And at that, they cannot go directly to the "top," but to a group called Central Facilities. This is a group of appointed men representing the major companies. They approve all important communications and recommendations. Their meetings are not public, although members of Town Council are permitted to attend some of them. So the feeling is that there are two areas of interest here, the operating companies and the public, with no link between them. In many cases, it is clear that decisions are made from the "business" view, such as refusing a Community Chest. Also, we feel that the Central Facilities is the stumbling block to getting to the Commission, since any reports we make must be submitted to them first. It is the hope that at least one public member be appointed to their board.

Some of the "higher uppers" have hinted that the people haven't taken much trouble to express themselves so they do what they think is best. The average person here is still very much under the influence of "secrecy." Very few are sure just how much can be said in public. I am not referring to anything scientific, but just ideas on everyday living. I am quite sure that most of the people feel that if they complain openly about anything, they will have the F.B.I. on their tails. This psychology persists not only with old-timers, but newcomers are impressed with it, too. (The favorite indoor sport at private gatherings is conjecturing on the way things are run here.) As far as anybody knows, no statement has ever been made that this is anything but an Army-run town; and when you think of Army, you think of strict supervision.

Most people are pinning their hopes on the Commission and there is a high feeling of confidence in the men on it.

Well, to get back to our "Survey." In addition to interviewing the heads of organizations, etc., we are starting to go into people's homes to get their reaction to a ready-made town, what they find here as compared to what they are accustomed to, what they anticipate for the future, etc. I am going out to the trailers tomorrow. Also have an appointment with the head of Recreation and Welfare. Incidentally, this setup is shrouded with mystery and has all sorts of rumors about it.

On the surface, Recreation and Welfare are supposed to be doing a marvelous job in meeting the needs of the community. Many of the social workers question their methods. Evidently, it is planned on a mass basis and individual groups or needs are not considered. There is a supposed discrepancy in the salaries of the workers—particularly social workers—and those in high positions. They question the qualifications of the workers and the rapid turnover. The recreation is on a hobby basis, rather than cultural.

Since the new housing company has taken over, we have been besieged by inspectors—sometimes two a day. The fence we put up five months ago came up for inspection today. Everything O.K., but we have no permit for it. So if I write them for a permit, they'll tell us it's all right to have built it. Oh yes, we have to paint it either white or green to conform to the "color scheme" of our house.

Dick was telling me the other day that the "caste" system at the plant even carries over into the lunchroom. The old-timer physicist or chemist eats with his own group every day. The groups depend on the positions they hold. The newcomers get up their own groups. I think most of the old ones feel like "big shots," and are very pompous. But I still can't figure it out. Our social position is rather doubtful, too. There are just a handful of men here on the staff of the University of Tennessee, and they all work part-time at the various plants. People like us are a problem. We don't exactly fit in anywhere, except that we have a little "in" with the Monsanto clique.

Oak Ridge does have a curious hold on people. I have heard similar statements from people living in all parts of town. They feel that they must get away every so often from the sameness of everything and the standardization. But they love to come back. And everyone will admit that a day's jaunt anywhere outside the gate is a big event. Even Irene notices the difference. We went shopping in a neighboring town, and she said, "This is a city, mummy." To a child, the difference may be the sidewalks and the concrete.

Dick appreciated the reprints that were sent to him and spent last night reading them. I hope to get [to] them soon. Big sigh.

Things look encouraging with the UN. We have been grateful to the Herald Tribune for news. There is hardly anything in the local papers except some scurrilous articles on Russia by Eugene Lyons. Mostly everybody has newspapers delivered from other cities. The N.Y. Times and P.M. have a wide circulation, and not especially to New Yorkers. There are a great many who don't subscribe to daily papers, but receive the Sunday editions.

We shall be leaving the "dear old South" next Wednesday, and expect to get to New York about the 21st for about ten days. I'll call you, and I hope we get to see each other.[1]

And so, until then

So long,
[sig] Thelma

P.S. Will you need "Small Town" before I see you? If so, I can easily send it.

---

[1] I did see Margaret; this was one of several meetings with her that we managed to arrange during frequent trips to New York. We had luncheon at the American Museum of Natural History. After the usual personal exchanges, we, naturally, discussed Oak Ridge. Always the teacher, she gave me some sound advice; briefing, or rather tutoring, me in simple methods for a laywoman in building up a background for "thinking sociologically." It was like having a private mini-course with her. In addition to scholarly books, she advised me to "read everything! Popular magazines like *Redbook*, *Ladies' Home Journal*, comic strips—even *True Confessions*—are important adjuncts in keeping up with current mores." (Years later, I repeated this advice to a young sociologist friend, Jane Weeks, who was teaching at the University of Tennessee. Just recently she told me that ever since then she has been instructing her students to do the same.)

The American Museum of Natural History
Central Park West at 79th Street
New York 24, N.Y.

January 9, 1947

Dear Thelma Present,

I've been thinking a lot about what you told me about the work that the Oak Ridge League of Women Voters is doing, and I mentioned it recently to one of the editors of the Ladies' Home Journal. It seems that the Journal is projecting an article on accomplishments of American communities and when your survey is finished and some of its results adopted, this would be very appropriate stuff for an article for them. I have given your name to Miss Hickey, and suggested that you would be able to give her the name of your chairman, and information as to how long the survey was likely to take, etc. I assume that you are keeping in touch with the work of the survey as a whole. It sounds like a significant and worthwhile project, going straight to the heart of our modern problem of how much planning we are to have in our lives, and what sorts of planning helps and what sort hinders the development of responsible civic behavior.

With best wishes to you and your husband,

Sincerely yours,
[sig] Margaret
Margaret Mead

Mrs. Richard Present,
518 Delaware Avenue,
Oak Ridge, Tenn.

72 Perry Street,
New York City
January 10, 1947

Dear Thelma,

I think the enclosure might kill two birds with one stone. It is of course designed for your chairman's eye, and also tells how the LHJ[2] project is going. It seems to me that will involve delay, so I plan to talk to some other people too. I am sending you "Middletown in Transition." I think that makes the three things I was to do. Did Dick see Compton's[3] article in the December Atlantic, the last paragraph is doing a lot of damage by throwing the whole thing out of scale.

Yours hastily,
[sig] Margaret

---

[2]*Ladies' Home Journal.*

[3]Dr. Arthur H. Compton.

After the war, Oak Ridge teemed with reporters and writers. Charmian revealed one incident:

> Years later, Pearl Buck was visiting Oak Ridge for material for a play she was writing about these scientists. She requested a meeting with only women present. I arranged a luncheon and had a hunch that Mrs. Buck wished to ask some very personal questions. She acted rather coy and hesitant (strange for a worldly authoress!); so I boldly asked just what she wanted to know. Even then Mrs. Buck requested her male secretary to phrase the question. It turned out that she wanted to know if there was much "hanky-panky" among the scientists during the war. The obvious answer was that most of them were just plain too exhausted because of the workload they carried.

Psychologist Lydia Bredig had explanations for the hold of Oak Ridge on the people there and what its aura of excitement did to their personal relationships:

> As I said, the emotional intensity was higher than it would have been among these people if they had been living in a more normal town. They fought more and they loved more. There was more openness of disagreement. There was more exchanging of sexual partners, for example. Many more women had affairs than they normally would have had. Mostly they stayed within their own peer group, but there were examples, particularly as the churches began to develop, where they met more in other groups and where they mixed more. Now maybe the exchange of sexual partners—and this I don't know, I can only give the impression—was greater among friendships in the laboratory between men and women than out in the community. I'm not sure of that. But I think that many more women, in finding themselves outside the intimacy, sought for it in other men; and then, also, in their need for expansiveness, they gave themselves more freedom in other ways. That would have to be documented; but that's my impression.
>
> All I can say as to when these relationships developed—from the beginning or as time went on—is that in some of the men, in 1947 when I first saw them at the laboratory, extramarital relationships were part of their problems. And the unmarried women who were working there were more concerned about sexual relationships with men who were married than they might have been in a less-structured community. I guess what I'm saying is that there was a greater intensity of funneling of emotions within the community—in a sense of being together and needing each other—and that it expressed itself sexually as it did in other ways. And that caused a lot of conflict, with a lot of guilt. This came out after I came to Oak Ridge. They had not been conscious of it at the time, but it was brewing.
>
> It would be hard to say what percentage of the problems was due to the secrecy of the town, or to its being a closed city, or to an uprooting from a former life and a difference in lifestyle, or everything put together. I would

say that the problems depended on what the individual was like before he came here, and what his fantasies and expectations were, and to what extent there was lack of support systems from family.

I think my experience is biased because I saw men who were unmarried basically because of their personal dynamics, and who tended to be quite rigid in their way of thinking and in their behavior, and who could not make the transition from a nuclear family to a family of their own. So a number of these men were much more insecure in personal relationships and could not handle the greater freedom of this community—the friendship freedom. They couldn't choose.

I probably had a biased sample, because a lot of people did choose. They chose partners they never would have chosen in another place. They went across cultural backgrounds; and some of them worked out very well, and some did not work out so well because the conflict of culture remained a basic in the new family.

The men, I would say, worked out better than the women, because the women seemed to have to bear more of the burden of the cultural change, unless they developed other aspects of themselves. They did not develop a personal self-esteem, for most of them were looking up to a husband. The opportunity for development came, of course, and that's what a lot of women did when they discovered talents in themselves that they may never have had before. The men developed, too, so that avocations were more intensely pursued, certainly in music and art and ways like that.

Since I had been a consultant in the schools working with the teachers, about a third or forty percent of my practice was with the children. Some of the children whom I saw came because of the conflict of the different cultures. Part of it was the conflict which happened elsewhere in the country, for there certainly was a change in the rest of the nation. But with a number of the parents, there was the pull toward achievement, and then there was the pull of permissiveness generally in the schools of the country. And then there was the pull of another very strong culture. I think the chief ingredient was the lack of intimacy between parents, which was reflected in more conflicts with many of the youngsters.

After the first exodus toward the end of '45 and in '46, husbands and wives had to face each other. Both had changed in subtle ways. The women had learned a great deal from each other, explored and explained their feelings of triumph, of gratification, of highs and lows and ambitions. And, most essentially, they had learned how to depend on themselves. Just as they had to decide whether to stay in Oak Ridge, they were faced with the decision of whether they wanted to stay married to their men who might seem more confident, interested in a wide range of activities, and who expected their wives to continue to help them.

Margaret Mead complained during her visit to Oak Ridge in 1964 that too many talented women were making bread. Well, they did a lot of other things beside bake bread. They organized the household; they started a number of women's groups; they began groups which studied government and politics, organized church activities, became artists, musicians and gardeners, and created the counterpart of the Renaissance man. During this, some marriages floundered, some men became childishly compulsive, some women secretly alcoholic and depressed. Most used their ingenuity and energy to grow. I feel that this is an important ingredient in why people stayed here. They stayed because they found a way and an acceptance and a sanction to do more than they had traditionally done. They had a chance to grow.

The talk about buying houses, and the opportunity to buy land and to buy new houses brought about profound changes. Buying or building a home introduced new dimensions not previously too important. How big a house? What would be in it? What do I really want? What kind of neighborhood? Who are the right people? And so on. Competitiveness between neighbors deepened, and anxieties about stability in work increased.

So the normalization of the city progressed. Wariness and the need to preserve territorial rights crept into the easiness of open and more generous relationships. Some people started worrying about whether they should have carpets, and then keeping them clean. Formality of relationships gradually increased. Instead of dropping in, some of us worried about the silver, preparing for a tea, a lunch, and what to wear. This process of formality tends to increase separation between groups and bring gradual rigidity within these groups. So what had been a spontaneous joy in inquiry and sharing has been developing into more ritualized methods of exchanges. The sense of MY way and THY way becomes stronger.

As I tried to explain this for myself, I had an image of brightly colored— some colors muted—swirling and touching ellipses, changing shape as they touched and rested, but in movement. And gradually the space narrowed. Some ellipses plopped and became still. Others continued to move and meet.

Letter XVIII

Oak Ridge, Tenn.
Jan. 24, 1947

Dear Margaret,

For a change, there is another upheaval in Oak Ridge since the announce-ment of the dismissals at TEC.[1] Unless those who were and are being let go find employment elsewhere on the area, they must leave within a very short time. Many of them have no place to go; there is great concern about taking childen out of school before the term is over; what to do about members of the family still working at other plants, etc. The other plants and companies are trying to absorb as many as they can. But the catch is, with Clinton Labs anyway, that any TEC people taking jobs with them will have to relinquish their permanent-type houses and be moved to a prefab or its equivalent to make way for others already on their waiting list. For many people that will be hard to take. Another story is that they will have to move if their incomes are less than $5,000 on their new jobs.

The latest stories I have been hearing about life here have been about some of the reactions of children. Some kids were discovered mutilating some trees and were reprimanded. The answer was, "What's the difference, it's only Government property!" A friend of mine found her children writing on the walls and when she scolded them, she got a similar response. Apparently it has reached such proportions that mothers have been invited to come to the schools and talk to the children about it. While on the subject of children, practically all I have spoken to say they love going to school here, as well as living here.

---

[1]Tennessee Eastman Corporation.

Reports are coming in steadily from our "survey." One of the most interesting was an investigation on the question of medical care. There has been a lot of dissatisfaction since the hospital was turned over to private practice, and one of our members interviewed all the doctors there. Many admitted that they are here because they have a house. The consensus is that there is not much of a future because of the rapid turnover here, and they are unwilling to remain in an unstable community. Further, because they must sign a yearly contract which may be revoked by the District Engineers, they are "not looking beyond a year of living" in Oak Ridge. They do not feel that they have the confidence of their patients. Since all their offices are in the hospital, they can see their patients "shopping" around. In this connection, there are some doctors at one of the plants who are interested in a plan of family medical care similar to what has been done in the Kaiser plant. They are trying to get the League and/or some other prominent groups to sponsor it.

The head of the Department of Health is trying to get a Board of Health started here. This is to be a lay group of people representing the various groups of residents—doctors, labor, women, etc. The League has been invited to appoint a member. The educators are also trying to start a Board of Education along the same lines, and they have approached us. We have heard of at least two more boards to be formed that are bidding for us. I don't mean to imply that we are the most popular organization here. But I have noticed so far that those people or groups of people that are actively civic-minded are approached for this and that.

Coincidentally, several of our League members had lunch at a cafe at the same time a group of teachers ate there. Those of us who had all eaten the same entree got ill from it, and immediately informed the management. We found out that this had happened to some of the teachers, and they were asked if they had reported it. (They belong to the Teacher's Group.) They said they were reluctant to make any complaints, give names and dates either as individuals or groups.

In all our interviews, everyone refers to the "Top" in hushed tones. The Army policy seems to be to have people do things and run things so as to relieve them of administrative details. But everyone knows they are the Boss. So no one is quite sure just how far they will be permitted to go. Nobody is quite sure who to go to for what, but we all know that the Army can make a sweeping edict that will affect hundreds of families at a moment's notice and that's that.

Your letter[2] was read at one of our committee meetings and was met with a lot of excitement. We plan to discuss it further and also await developments. I am fairly certain that something can be done with the idea, especially if something tangible comes up.

Every other woman seems to be pregnant around here. They sure go in for much larger families. Almost everyone I know has at least two children, but I have not known so many of the professional class to have three, four or more.

---

[2]Jan. 29, 1947, with reference to the League of Women Voters.

Along other lines, it is amazing what you find yourself doing in a place like this. After trying my hand at cookies, I have so far created two cakes. But don't you dare tell me I'll be baking bread next. Even though Dick says my cakes surpass anything he has tasted, I would be very happy to be able to run into Sutters for their yummy things.

I have started visiting families at the trailer camp. The interiors are appalling. There are single and double ones. None of them have running water, but several women boasted of electricity. All the water has to be carried from the central water supply. The women are tied down all day just keeping their houses and families clean and fed. And yet, without exception, when asked how they liked Oak Ridge the answer was, "I like it fine." Of course, one would rather be nearer the wash house, or have a better drainage system, or be nearer a playground, or get rid of some of "those people with their goings-on," but otherwise they really seemed quite cheerful. When asked if they intended to remain, most of them said it depended on how long their husband's job would last. We have just started these personal interviews and hope to get a crew of women to cover all the key areas in town.

Thanks for sending the book. The longer I live here, the more I marvel at Granville Hicks being able to turn out any work. Things sure do pile up in a "Small Town." Just imagine, I just got around to reading "Balinese Character,"[3] and that is just one of the reasons I haven't written sooner. I couldn't put it down. The treatment is excellent, and the whole book fascinating.

We both enjoyed seeing you on our last trip and hope you will be coming this way soon.

Bye now,
[sig] Thelma

---

[3]*Balinese Character*, written by Gregory Bateson and Margaret Mead. A fascinating study. Gregory presented Dick with a copy before our leaving New York City.

Letter XIX

Oak Ridge, Tenn.
March 8, 1947

Dear Margaret,

Today marks our first anniversary in Oak Ridge. This realization was pointed up by two incidents. After a meeting of the League of Women Voters a few nights ago, I spoke to a newcomer here and asked her impression of the meeting, which was concerned with local affairs, etc. She said she felt as if she were in a strange country where they spoke a foreign language. I remember what a mystery such expressions as "Rec & Welfare," "the Hill," "district engineer," "USED," "perms," "prefabs" and such were to me at first.

Then we attended the Oak Ridge Symphony, and I found that my reaction was quite different. I was far more tolerant of the performance, so pleased at the large attendance and even proud of our O.R. citizens who had the will to stick together and produce a Haydn symphony for us.

Our Survey, which was going along at a great pace, has been slowed down considerably. I think it is on the verge of being strangled. After gathering quantities of material and facts, we find that we are unable to make much use of the stuff, except for a few innocuous instances. The "Boys" on the "Hill" seem to consider our findings dynamite. However, we have been feeding a lot of it to Town Council and perhaps in the long run it will be effective. Personally, I believe that many of us were intimidated by rumors about the survey. Some of the stories were that a group of Reds were trying to discredit some things around here; the doctors claimed they were outraged by our insinuations; others claimed that we were using the information for sheer gossip.

One of our most valuable functions is to build up Town Council and make it truly representative of the people. Several members of the council are very sincere in their efforts to bring this about, and several committees have been formed, including recreation, education, health, etc., and members consist of representatives of prominent civic organizations—ours, too.

Since T.E.C. has practically closed down, several important citizens are leaving. Overheard at a council meeting, "Too bad so and so is leaving. We're losing a good man. We need to build up others to replace those leaving." There are several clippings on the appointment of the leading citizens by Kiwanis. Many people consider Oak Ridge a most democratic town because anybody can rise to a prominent position in civic affairs. (Provided they are not too pink.) At a farewell party given by T.E.C. to which families were invited, one of the counselors employed there was referred to as a "big-talkin' woman."

The Commission almost got started on the wrong foot. It seems they wrote for arrangements to be made for offices for the architects who were going to plan their buildings. Without warning, and no one is quite sure who is responsible for the orders, all the residents of three dormitories were given notice to evacuate in a week, and were given a list of vacancies in the worst part of town. As I have written, conditions in the dorms at their best are on a low level, and this has been a minor scandal. Those who got the notices feel this to be an infringement on civil rights or sumpin', and they have threatened to leave. The outcome will depend on the action the companies take in behalf of their employees affected.

A meeting was called at Clinton Lab with one of the heads and those affected by the order, but nothing has come of it and nothing much is expected. According to one of the secretaries, the single people here feel the only consideration in the Oak Ridge setup is for married people, and they feel quite out of the picture. A few talk of some kind of organization concerning their housing welfare, but for the majority there is too much at stake. Quite a number put up with conditions because they have a good opportunity to get their degrees while earning a living; others have no degrees and yet are doing the kind of work where one would be required elsewhere; some are earning more money than they have ever gotten; and I suppose some find the living conditions much better than they have ever had.

Speaking of meetings, one of our young scientists (a member of AORES[1]) was scheduled to address a CIO group in Oak Ridge. He works for Monsanto, incidentally, and was visited by one of the big chiefs before his talk. The latter had received a call from another big chief at Carbide who was in a dither for fear he might discuss labor relations. At the end of the discussion, the scientist recommended that they both forget it ever took place—adding that he was confident that there was no censorship on public talks.

We were surprised to discover that the head of the Public Health Department had no authority to close down any public eating places that were substandard without permission from the Army. However, if it were possible

---

[1]Association of Oak Ridge Engineers and Scientists.

to have the head of the department appointed by the state, he could then go over their heads (the Army's).

Following are some passing and totally unrelated reflections:

—Haven't read or heard of any burials here.

—The Western type movies are the most popular.

—Negroes are required to get an extra permit for all visitors—one from the colored Hutment camp manager and then from Town Hall.

—All applicants for jobs are still investigated, but by F.B.I. now, rather than military intelligence. (Except for red tape, most people are glad about it—feel more secure about trusting people here.)

—Excellent traffic system and vehicle inspection. All cars must pass a test for safety for which a red sticker is given. Constant campaign for safety in driving results in hardly any accidents and none fatal.

—Just discovered we have a jail here that has never been used. Some law prohibits the locking of prison doors, and in order to use it, would have to have guards.

—More and more talk about "thank God for the gates—otherwise would have to lock doors, and undesirables would invade our grounds for picnics, shop here and use our facilities."

—Hardly ever hear of divorces or marital scandals in residential area.

—A popular question, "How long are you staying here?"

—A popular answer, "Haven't any idea."

—More and more people leaving. More and more coming in. A feeling of nostalgia when someone tells you they are leaving.

—Never saw so many raffles or a more organized place.

—Regimentation of thought and action.

—A Monsanto wife refers to another woman's husband, not employed there, as "her husband not our type."

And so

Good night,

[sig] Thelma

Dorm discontent was nothing new. For some it was a long winter of perpetual discontent; for others this crude living was no more disconcerting than the showers that must come with spring.

Herbert Pomerance rolled in from Chicago with the punches and adapted a dorm to himself as easily as he adapted to a dorm. In his interview, he said:

> I left Chicago the Saturday after Thanksgiving in 1943, stopped off to see a friend somewhere else, and got into Knoxville Monday morning. So my first sight of Knoxville was at 6:30 A.M. in the pawnshop area.[2]
>
> I had to spend half a day in the Knoxville employment office checking in. It

---

[2]Both the Southern Railway and L&N Railroad stations were near North Gay Street in Knoxville, not one of the city's better downtown areas.

all had to start from there, and I had to get a pass, too. Then I had three days in the Oak Ridge hotel until I could get a dorm assignment, and I shared a room with a Columbia University professor who was active in the project, an engineer.

I came as a chemical analyst. I'd been in spectroscopy in physics and had asked to be an assistant in the courses in analytical spectroscopy at the University of Chicago, so when I was hired, it was in analytical spectroscopy.

(How did you get the job? —*T.P.*)

Anyone who was at the University of Chicago was available to the project there because they were known directly. Actually, I had to get permission from the Radiation Lab at MIT where I had tentatively accepted a post, and I had to write them, saying that the people in Chicago believed that they could make more of my talent, to get a release.

The man I had worked for in that training course was already in the project, so what better way than that he should ask for me. So I worked at the University for a year in the spectroscopy lab, then back to Chicago for half a year. The spec lab in Chicago was the spec lab for all the chemical analysts in the project. One man went out to Hanford, Washington, one went to Los Alamos, New Mexico, one to K-25 here, and I was the one who set up the lab at X-10. I was doing thesis work for a physics degree, so what they did was hire me as though I was a Ph.D.

I came to Oak Ridge as a professional man, but since housing was based on family size, I had a dorm room. And, for that matter, so did some Army officers. The man next to me for months was a major.

(What was your reaction when you arrived in Oak Ridge? To the gates and passes? —*T.P.*)

Well, we were accustomed to the passes in Chicago and the companionship in the laboratory. I was in the lab here only a couple of hours when quitting time came because I had been in Knoxville checking in. A fellow I had supper with said, "I'm going up to see a friend of mine who is ill and staying at the house of someone who is taking care of him." So I went up, too, and started right in on the social life.

The social life was that every door was open. I can remember I could leave somebody's house at 11:30 and halfway down the hill to the dorm say, "Well, these people don't go to bed until 2:00, I'll just drop in." The companionship was not based on organizations then. Now it's based on church or on some clubs you might belong to. But in those days the lab would have a dance for everybody at the lab—machinists and scientists together. So we knew everybody at the lab and could be quite social with them.

(Were you socially connected with those outside the lab? Did you visit in the homes of people who were not in the scientific community? —*T.P.*)

Well, those of us in the dorms had no way of inviting anybody in. I couldn't invite my mother into my room. The rules were very strict, even worse than college dorms. There was a lounge on the first floor opposite the desk clerk and that was the only place a person of the opposite sex could come in, except the cleaning ladies. So it meant I couldn't entertain my parents at the dorm. I had to entertain them at some friend's house—somebody who was married and had a child and so was eligible for a house—or go out somewhere. Most of us didn't have cars; we rode to the lab on the buses, or we could walk. But it was no trick to go anywhere. Even after Ellie and I were married, I didn't have a car for awhile. And when I had to go to orchestra rehearsal, I'd see my bus coming over the hill, take my cello and walk out and catch it at the corner and go to rehearsal that way.

So it meant we could go anywhere, and we had plenty of activities. The first day I was here, I saw a mimeographed *Journal* announcing these activities. There was an announcement that anyone who could play a stringed instrument should go around to the high school, Room Something, on Tuesday evening and that was how I met Jacinta Howard. She was sitting there, and that's how we cooked up a quartet to play at the first Christmas here. On my second evening in Oak Ridge, I had already gotten in with the orchestra.

We worked six days a week, so that meant we didn't have Saturdays to go to the Smokies. If we went, it had to be Sundays. Even after the war, they once measured the working time of the people at our lab. Some Army officer wanted anyone who came in after 8:00 to sign in for being late. So the lab director said, "Well, if they have to sign in late, they ought to be able to sign out late, too." So they had a record of how much time people were spending at the lab. It turned out that the professional staff was working fifty-four hours a week for a forty-eight-hour week.

But if you lived in a dorm, you had to eat in a cafeteria. The central cafeteria at Townsite served fourteen dorms the first year, and then when they built several more in the area, they served about eighteen—one hundred forty residents per dorm. They served twenty-four hours a day. When they started double bedding in the dorm rooms, it was more than that.

There were no facilities for even making a cup of coffee. No place to keep a thing cold. After the war when the dorm population dropped—or maybe even during the war—there were some fellows who had end rooms which were double rooms, and they arranged somehow to get bunks so they could have four fellows in one room and have the other double room as a club room, and they put in a refrigerator to hold their chocolates and beer.

My aunt sent me cookies, and the red ants were so numerous that I had to fix a moat so that the ants couldn't come into the cookie box.

A fellow who wanted to practice the piano could not get a piano in. But I could practice my cello.

The people who were brought into Oak Ridge were too young to have many high school-age children. The high school population was two hundred or so—small. So where did you get baby-sitters? You got them from the staff you worked with. You asked the secretary in your section, and you didn't really know if you should pay her. So you invited her for dinner. The dinner was the pay; she didn't have to eat in the cafeteria.

One friend who was a lab assistant was newly married. He had a house or an apartment assignment, but the place wasn't finished and he had to wait for it to be completed, wait about three months. He and his wife had to live in separate dorms, where, as I said, the opposite sex couldn't come past the desk. So his chief would invite George to come baby-sit.

"Look, George," he'd say. "We're going out. The baby goes to sleep to 7:30. Why don't you and your wife come up and take care of the baby. We're not coming back until 11:00. We'll make a lot of noise when we come up the steps." So that was another way to get baby-sitters.

The professional staff also baby-sat, and I did some, too. Of course, there was the problem that you couldn't pay such a person. All they could do was say, "Look, you can have a party. We have a big record collection and you can serve Cokes and cookies." And we would have brought beer.

(What were the physical facilities in the dorms? Were they well-maintained and clean? —T.P.)

The rooms were built on a module of 8 x 12 feet, so the rooms were that size, minus the thickness of the walls. I had one bed, one dresser, one chair and a little bitty closet. I had got hold of some lumber somewhere and had built a bookcase. We had daily maid service, a community shower, and it was still free enough of theft that, although we had to learn to lock our rooms going to the shower, we were likely to take the key with us.

But at night we would leave the doors open for cross ventilation. I had to learn that I couldn't leave the window in my room open during the day because of thundershowers which would come in and wet everything there. The only time I remember dirt on my bed was when the rain washed in through the window screen. We had coal-fired heat and Oak Ridge was pretty sooty.

There was a central laundry close to the central cafeteria, and we had about one-week service. Dry cleaning was more irregular. Once Y-12 had an accident and needed a lot of solvent to clean up the equipment, so they sequestered all the dry cleaning fluid and that really slowed it down.

After the war, or near the end, I wrote a letter to the Army saying, "The women's dorms have Bendix washing machines. You ought to be fair to us and let us have them too." We wanted to wash our socks and things. A girl I knew who worked there (for the Army) told me later that it was treated as a "damn fool letter" from some nut. But when they began closing dorms after the war, when so much of the population had left, they had Bendix machines left over and they put them in the men's dorms. Before that I would take my clothes to the laundry, but my socks I washed myself in the basin and hung them up on a string to dry.

(Did you live in a dorm until you married? —T.P.)

No, I was out of the dorm twice. Right after the war, a couple went back to school. He needed three months and she six for bachelor's degrees, and he already had a two-bedroom apartment with a friend living there. So when he and his wife went to college, two more of us chemists or physicists moved in. But I had to move back to the dorm when they came back.

Then a year later they had a surfeit of various housing—E apartments, some East Village flattops and also some D houses. They didn't have enough families needing three bedrooms, so some of the D houses became what were called D house dorms and six single people (of the same sex) could live together. And those people could get together and hire a housekeeper who'd come in at noon, clean up the place and cook supper for them. That was one of the deals. I think the girls did their own cooking. I didn't choose to go in one, but applied for an E apartment which I could have if I brought in two others with me, and I lived in that for a year until I got married.

Letter XX

Oak Ridge, Tenn.
April 12, 1947

Dear Margaret,

Our one sprig of forsythia bloomed this week, and I came down with spring fever—a mild case, no temperature.

There has been almost a complete turnover of tenants on our street. Practically all of our neighbors, formerly of T.E.C., have moved—some into prefabs and others leaving the area. There is a moving van on the street every day and it is somewhat depressing. Our next door neighbor switched over to Monsanto from T.E.C., found the adjustment too difficult and is quitting. There is a great deal of resentment of both sides—in the engineering divisions anyway. Some T.E.C. men were put in higher positions than Monsanto people who had been employed there for a while. T.E.C. people don't like unions (they voted "no union") and rebel at joining. Monsanto is AFL. I have heard of similar unhappy situations in some secretarial departments. In spite of dissatisfactions, people stay here because salaries are pretty good and, more important, is the question of housing.

Many things have happened recently, or rather come to light, that have made living here rather discouraging. More and more one hears we are getting the "disadvantages of any normal town with none of the advantages."

Now, when we wish to get passes for visitors, we must sign a slip to the effect that our guest is not an alien, writer, radio commentator, investigator, etc.—a long list. Not everyone takes it too seriously. The same thing was required during the war.

Talking about passes, I just discovered that in addition to having to get permission for a pass for visitors from the manager of the colored Hutments, the Negroes were required to pay $1.50 for each pass. Finally one was heard

159

grumbling about it at Town Hall, where we get our regular passes, and it was investigated and stopped. However, any Negro's visitor staying overnight or more is required to pay rent at Hutment rates. This applies to anyone living in Victory Cottages even if they have extra room. One colored maid was expecting her father for a visit with the expectation that he might find work here. But whether he works or not, he will have to pay rent. They claim that everyone here is supposed to be working and therefore must pay for lodging.

Another incident at the camp has enraged many of us. Originally, all Hutments were furnished with blankets and sheets by the Army. At one time there was a surplus which was sold to families in Victory Cottages. Mr. ———— decided that unless they (the Negroes) could produce receipts of their purchase, they could be confiscated as stolen goods. So he sent people to search the houses (no warrants), while they were out. I know of one maid who couldn't find her receipt and burned her blanket and sheet rather than have it confiscated. Well, a group of whites are investigating, but have little hope of getting any satisfaction.

A lot of women would like to augment their incomes by having some type of small business in their home. Verboten! There is something in our contract that says nix.

There are all sorts of regulations about starting businesses with specific qualifications required. Yet one hears of an Army colonel being a silent partner with a son of a Roane-Anderson man. The latter has none of the required qualifications.

More gripes about the hospital. Rates are going up—$6 per day for a ward room. Most people here have hospitalization. This arrangement is made by the hospital with the companies. The boy next door who had been working at T.E.C. and was waiting for clearance to start at Monsanto, was seized suddenly with an appendicitis attack and operated upon. Because he wasn't working at any of the companies at the time, he had to pay full rate. We feel lucky to have the Blue Cross plan, but very few people know about it or care.

There is an Army doctor who performs a rare ulcer operation, but he is not permitted to treat civilians. The man across the street had it done. His wife told me it was only because they knew some very prominent people who used their influence.

We have a short faucet on our sink which breaks my (and Dick's) back when washing dishes. I called the Oak Ridge Housing months ago, and was referred higher and higher up. Then I was told I had to write a letter to get action. This I did. Then they sent some plumber around and an investigator who OK'd it. I think they are going to ask for a doctor's certificate next.

Socially, it's about on the same level. The scientists talk about nothing but atomic energy from the political side. They feel pretty futile and you hear the same things over and over again. I hardly ever look forward to gatherings. We know exactly what will be discussed, and while everybody complains about it and tries to change the subject, eventually the men come back to it. Dick says bull sessions always used to wind up with a discussion of sex or religion, now it's atomic energy.

In spite of the fact that Town Council tries to center its meetings around pertinent questions, the attendance hasn't increased. The teen-agers, however, put up a solid front at the meeting concerned with the operation of Rec & Welfare. Some of us in the LWV urged our board to prepare a resolution to be presented for a vote that we have at least one representative of the civilian population appointed to the council of R&W. (As it is now, the members are appointed by the companies.) But there was the usual hesitation about taking action for fear of stepping on this or that one's toes. Well, these kids came en masse, like a debating team, and demanded that prices be lowered for them at the movie houses. They were righteous, insistent and unafraid. What's more, they were taken seriously. The chairman commended them on their turnout, but asked, "Why aren't your parents here?"

An old law, made in 1870, which has not been put into practice for many years and which requires payment of a personal property tax, was suddenly sprung on the county (including Oak Ridge). Everybody was up in arms, so Town Council called a meeting. The hall was packed—with people standing. We were advised publicly and not too subtly to break the law. It takes an ancient law that hits the pocketbook to get people to a town meeting. The advice was to conceal assets and undervalue property.

Lately, however, the Oak Ridge Journal has been carrying many more letters to the editor. Most of them were complaints on one thing or another. There has been talk that the paper was to be enlarged and there will be a 10-cent charge. Of course, nobody thought to find out how many people would buy it at any price. Much as the people wish it, there doesn't seem to be any possibility of having a daily paper here with regular news coverage.

A lot of people who moved from the area like to save their badges as souvenirs. Some like to hold on to them so that they can get in again whenever they want. Everybody who works here has a work badge which is turned in when they are terminated. They are then given a temporary pass which gives them the same privileges as a guest. If they don't get a job within thirty days, they must leave. There is no possibility of their keeping their badges. My neighbor, who has worked here three years, is now a guest in his own house. Housewives, on the other hand, have resident badges which they keep until they move. My neighbor's wife is going to have her son get her a guest pass which she will show as she leaves the gate, and will keep her badge.

When Negroes are terminated, they are allowed only one week's temporary pass to try to find work. Further, they are required to pay $4.50 for it. When they are behind in rent, they must pay 50 cents a day for each day they delay.

There is a clipping enclosed for Gregory from Dick. He also sends regards.

Bye, now,
[sig] Thelma

Letter XXI

Dear Margaret,

What with German measles, impetigo and a new unhousebroken puppy, my correspondence is in arrears.

The last Town Council meeting had about only ninety people attending, and the size of the audience was discouraging. The subject up for discussion was the proposed new constitution, and it turned into a lively and heated meeting. Enclosed you will find an account of it. The thing that really pepped it up was a resolution to the Commission asking for real citizen participation. It was the first time that anything came up that had any teeth in it and was voted almost unanimously. Then there were several points in the constitution that were debated seriously.

The residents jammed the hall and overflowed into several meeting places with loudspeakers the night Lilienthal[1] spoke. He made a favorable impression, but didn't say anything of particular significance.

The Army is out of control now (although the personnel is the same in many positions yet), but so far there has not been much evident change except for the worse in some cases. But there are optimists who say it will get worse here before it gets better. For example, Rec & Welfare seems to be losing ground. We had an interview with the president of the R&W council, and he seemed quite bitter toward the AEC. They are getting less sources for funds and have to curtail many activities. He said the companies will be the only ones to have any weight with the Commission, [that] the civilians will have even less to say,

---

[1]David E. Lilienthal, chairman of the Atomic Energy Commission.

163

and that Town Council is just a sop. Many think that eventually the AEC will
take over R&W, as they don't believe the setup is working out to the best
interest of the people, and the above remarks are sour grapes.

A representative from the AEC came here to talk things over with several
groups and particularly asked to meet with some members of the LWV. He
said they were impressed with our reports on the survey and activities locally,
and that we seemed to be the only group seriously interested in the future of
Oak Ridge government. He felt that we should have an uncensored paper
except for news dealing with security, and in general more representation of
the people.

Turnover is still going on on a large scale. Someone I know said she is just
going through her third set of friends. I think housing is keeping at least half
of the population here.

The wife of the head of the physics department at Monsanto has a mania for
organizing. One of the physicist's wives had a baby and was in the hospital. I
know her rather well and planned to visit her. In the meantime, the department head's wife called all the other wives to organize their visits to the
hospital for specific days and hours. She, herself, went to the hospital and
found one woman there who was supposed to be there on another day and
berated her for it. The poor new mother was utterly exhausted by the time
she was ready to leave.

Monsanto has not received a new contract yet, and there is a lot of
speculation and unrest—at least among the scientists—as to their jobs and
the future of Oak Ridge.

One day some Monsanto women were gossiping about Mrs. _____. They
were amused at her airs and that she considered herself "elite." So I asked
who really made up the elite here. One said, "We are, of course."

This is picnic time in Oak Ridge and is the most popular form of recreation.
Many people have outdoor equipment in back of their houses, and there are
also some beautiful spots outside the area. Every other person you meet
complains of backache from gardening, which almost amounts to a mania
around here.

Practically everyone is being reinvestigated by the FBI as well as new
applicants for jobs. Just another subject for speculation, gossip and insecurity.

One of the women on the block was kind enough to have a neighborhood
tea. I would liked to have gone, because in more than a year I've gotten to
know hardly anyone around here, but I couldn't make it. A few days later I
met someone a few houses down and asked her how it turned out. She said,
"Oh, it was all right, but imagine, she used fiesta ware!"

We had a flat one night and couldn't use the car. We tried to get a hitch and
almost a dozen cars passed us by. Because it was late and we were tired, Dick
and I felt that this was one of the most unfriendly and heartless towns we
knew. A popular remark is, "This is a town where children and dogs are
happy—anyway."

No doubt you read the article on Oak Ridge in the New York Times several weeks ago by Cabbell Phillips.[2] It was excellent.

Irene has temperature again, and the pup just puddled on our best rug.

Hastily yours,
[sig] Thelma

P.S. I hope I didn't scare you off when I mentioned requirements for passes in one letter. It doesn't really mean anything.

72 Perry Street
Between 4th and Bleeker
New York City
Chelsea 3-8236 or Watkins 9-1716

June 26, 1947

Dear Thelma,

I've been a bad correspondent this spring and a disappointed one too, because we are sad that we never got down to visit you before we got off for Europe. Now with sailing looming on Monday, all I can do is say good-bye until fall. If you think you are more likely to write your letters if they are mailed regularly do mail them—they will be carefully filed away. Otherwise keep a journal for me until I come back, and surely next year I will somehow get down.

Yours,
[sig] Margaret

---

[2]"Oak Ridge Ponders Its Clouded Future," C. Phillips, N.Y. *Times Magazine*, pp. 12-13, April 13, 1947.

Letter XXII

Dear Margaret,

I got back to Oak Ridge [from New York] in time to take part in the raging controversy about the Information meeting. This is one of the big events of the season where scientists gather from all the projects—about 150 were expected. Naturally the women were all agog, and endless arguments ensued as to the best procedure for entertaining the visitors. The big question was whether to have separate parties for physicists, chemists, etc., or one big one. Well, the big party won, and committees of wives were set up. One woman raised a terrific row because the physicists' wives were overstaffed in proportion to the number of physicists, and claimed that the chemistry department would be insulted. The punch committee took their assignment seriously and had a swell time. They met every afternoon for a week and sampled drinks (spiked, of course).

A Dance Club was formed last spring. Members are voted in and there is a waiting list. It was started ostensibly to give those who liked to dance the opportunity to do so about once a week. Apparently they now admit only those "types" that "fit in." One young matron said she would be happy if she could just make the waiting list.

I have been invited to become a member of a committee of laymen to investigate certain welfare problems and to make recommendations to the board of the Family Service Bureau. There are two pressing needs. One is the demand for Homemaker's Service, and the other is the need for foster homes on a long-term basis. At present Nesper House is equipped to handle emergency care, but they do not accept infants, as they require too much individual care. Nesper House is rendering a desperately needed service,

167

but, of course, it is an institution. When they are filled, they cannot possibly give the children much personal attention. For short-term care, it is considered adequate. However, the Family Service Bureau feels that many children cannot adjust to institution life even for a short spell, and so want to investigate the possibilities of foster homes and to build up the Homemaker Service which has already been established.

Both present problems here. Because of the setup in housing, there is usually little or no extra space, although assuredly there are many families who would be willing to foster children. Their reasons might be practical, or altruistic, or both.

One solution would be for the authorities to accept applications for larger houses than a family might ordinarily need, if they specified their intent to become foster parents and lived up to it. Could the authorities be made to see the need?

Right now there are about six Homemakers on call. None are practical nurses and only one takes confinement cases. These women must be recruited from the area and are not permitted to live here on the basis of Homemaker service alone, but must be supported by someone employed here. There are a few other women here who do this work free-lance, so to speak. One of these has a serious heart condition, and the FSB will not enroll her. Another woman will only work in the very best type of home. The FSB has also investigated these women who advertise in the Journal to "keep" children by the day, and found that practically all of them are unsuited for the work. Either conditions are unsanitary, food meagre, or they take too many children at one time.

Most of the requests for these two services come from men whose wives have left home, and working mothers. In most confinement cases where there are older children, the families either import a grandmother or send their children on visits. One of our recommendations is to request the authorities to permit women to come here to live having as their means of livelihood the Homemaker Service. Well, it will be interesting to see what the board will say to all this and if these problems will go to the AEC.

Speaking of the AEC reminds me that security is getting even tighter than when the Army was in control. They are particularly watchful about aliens. I applied for a pass for my piano tuner with a German-sounding name. I was questioned as to whether or not he was an alien and if he was a citizen. But something more serious than that, Dick has a Chinese graduate student in Knoxville. He registered in one course that Dick is giving in the extension school in Oak Ridge. He attended a few classes and then told Dick that his pass was taken away. And his case has to be considered in Washington. If he will not be permitted to come here, this will mean, effectively, that no foreign students will be able to get a degree in physics at the University of Tennessee because—the staff being too small to give the same graduate courses at both places—it would take a prohibitive amount of time for a student to take the necessary courses in Knoxville alone.

The latest social developments:

Newest forms of entertaining is having a Coffee Party at 10:30 A.M. Best bibs and tuckers are worn.

The Dance Club is admitting five more couples as new members. Fourteen names were nominated out of the applications, and a secret ballot was sent to all members with instructions to vote for five and to consider carefully the most desirable—underlined three times.

Two of our young, ambitious matrons decided to pay an impromptu call one afternoon on a woman with most "desirable" connections. Upon their arrival, a maid informed them she was resting. When they pressed her to find out when it would be convenient to return, she was very vague. Before leaving reluctantly, each of the callers opened their purses and left their calling cards, another new touch. Since they had time to spare, they decided to show themselves off at the busiest market. A few minutes later, they saw Mrs. _____ drive up to a nearby bus stop and let the maid, who was sitting next to her, get out. She then went into the store to market, but not before the other two made a hasty retreat to their car.

The division head of engineering at Monsanto just moved to a D house. This is the largest type of house. They have no children. Now the wife of the chemical division head (also childless) feels the need of a D house because of their social position and prestige.

Mrs. _____, who created a stir when she took her child back and forth from nursery school by cab, has caused further comment by taking a taxi to Knoxville once a week for shopping.

Finally read the article in Life by Gorer which I enjoyed, but I think he got most of his information from Mead's book, "And Keep Your Powder Dry."

All packages sent and received here are opened for inspection.

We have had a small boarder two years of age for several days. His mother is in the hospital. The parents had considered sending the child to Nesper House, but their doctor hinted that there had been some epidemics there because they had not inspected the children carefully enough. Fortunately, they knew us well enough to feel free to ask us to help out.

We have arrived! Dick has been invited to become a member of the board of directors of the Oak Ridge Civic Music Association.

The "New Look" is gradually seeping into Oak Ridge, and slacks are on the wane.

And so to bed.

G'night,
[sig] Thelma

Letter XXIII

Dear Margaret,

We took a short trip to Florida over the Xmas holiday and missed the first part of the excitement that struck Oak Ridge like a hurricane.

No doubt, you read of the changes that are taking place here. From what I've seen in out-of-town papers, it all sounds like a simple and natural move of the AEC. However, the suddenness and surprise of their actions had such an impact here that it seemed as if the very bottom had fallen from the city.

All Oak Ridge was preparing for the New Year's festivities with parties, dances, parties and parties, when the day before, the announcement came that the contract with [University of Chicago] Chicago University to take over Monsanto had been withdrawn and was to be given to Carbide. No one at Clinton Lab had been consulted, and the effect on the men was a terrible shock. They all felt their insignificance and like pawns that could be pushed to any part of the country at the will of the AEC. All one could hear was that AEC stinks, Lilienthal stinks, Carbide stinks. In fact, there isn't a breath of fresh air in Oak Ridge.

The men (scientists) were ready to resign en masse, meetings were called, negotiations went on for weeks in the hope that the decision could be changed. There were countless calls and visits to Washington, and even Truman was appealed to, but the decision stands. Then, there was the faint hope that at least a director would be appointed [who] would be acceptable to the scientists. Several good men were approached, and finally one man who had their respect said he would consider the appointment subject to certain provisions that would give the scientists some security. He was turned down on every point. So now the men are all looking for jobs and everyone talks of leaving at the earliest opportunity.

Aside from the men at the Lab, the whole city has felt it. The businessmen cried it was a plot of the North against the South, that this was Lilienthal's revenge at McKellar. [1] The churches are wondering what's going to happen to their congregations. And so it goes. The man at the frozen meat locker said he had six cancellations in one day.

It's all rather ironic because Oak Ridge really seemed to be settling down. There was a feeling of stability and permanence. There was, and still is, talk of expansion. Plans are being made for more housing, permanent church buildings. The Oak Ridge radio station was inaugurated last Sunday; the Journal is going on a subscription basis or on sale at five cents a copy.

The League of Women Voters has almost disintegrated. The membership was predominantly Clinton Lab wives, and no one wants to accept any office. The usual reason is, "May be leaving any day."

This past week practically all the physicists left town to attend the American Physical Society meetings in New York. The majority went hoping either to land a job or make contacts for one. So the wives had all kinds of hen parties. Fortunately, the weather was treacherous and I had to cancel some of the supper engagements. After attending a few where the conversation centered on babies, furnaces, husbands and recipes, a hermit's life was most appealing. The women have a round of people they call at least once a day. "Hi, what's new?" One girl complained to me today that she didn't really mind when her "closest" friend always asked her who and where she visited, or who was at so-and-so's house, but it now has reached the point where she asks who has called her on the phone.

The enlarged Journal [has] a society page now. It is, of course, the most popular addition. I'm still trying to dope out just what "Society" means here. It seems to me that almost anyone can get to be a prominent person here if they just work at it. You join any organization that appeals to you, and become active. It's always easy to become an officer, because there is always some vacancy to be filled. Newcomers have a good chance of going far in any club. They usually join to make contacts (social), and because they are so anxious and willing, they are nabbed. But, because of the turnover here, the many company factions, the overwhelming number of organizations, there doesn't seem to be any one "select group." There are possibly three or four names of top men that one remembers for more than a few months. I guess the church is the one place one could find a cross-section of the population, and aside from that, everyone moves in his own little orbit.

Culturally, there has been real progress. There is now an organized music group. We have managed to get some good artists here at our own expense, and there is a real demand for good music. There is talk of organizing sufficient numbers to warrant bringing foreign movies or good revivals. And speaking of revivals, the Community Chorus is producing "The Merry Widow." But the conductor decided it was too risque and might offend some people, so has revised one or two scenes. In place of the can-can, I believe

---

[1] Sen. Kenneth D. McKellar, a Tennessee Democrat from Memphis.

they are doing some pretty waltzes, and instead of drinking wine, tea will be served. This will be a unique production.

The board of the Family Service Bureau showed definite interest in the proposal to try to arrange for Homemakers to be on a payroll as regular employees and thus be eligible for housing. A study is being made to find out how this works in other communities, as to salaries, hours, etc.

Our "second" shows every evidence of being on its way (end of April) to the extent of pushing me farther and farther away from the typewriter and piano keys.

We tuned in on our local radio station one morning. The main feature from 6 to 9 A.M. is "Up'N'Atom." Inevitable.

We hope you have all been well this winter. Dick sends regards.

As ever,
[sig] Thelma

Waldo Cohn had this to say about the beginnings and development of music in Oak Ridge and of the outstanding artists who were brought in:

A notice appeared in the weekly, one-page, Army-run announcement sheet about the possible formation of instrumental groups, mentioning a designated place in the high-school music room, and that interested persons should appear. Jacinta Howard and I were the only string instrumentalists there that night, and we formed the first chamber music group. More and more amateur musicians wanted to play, and soon the numbers were too large to meet in our home.

There was, originally, an abundance of brass players, and I suggested that they form a band. Gradually enough string, wind and other players appeared to make an orchestra a possibility. Originally, we met for practice with my leading from my cello position. But many of the musicians could not see me from their posts, and I was requested to stand up and become the formal conductor. I soon recognized that the orchestra could not become full-fledged without financial assistance. Music stands, scores and more instruments—for example, kettle drums and the like—were needed for those players who had not (or could not have) brought their instruments with them.

I went to the R&W with an itemized request for $800. This came through, and so from beer and movies, Oak Ridge had a bona fide orchestra. The first public performance was given November 4, 1944, with sixty-five musicians from twenty-three different states and all walks of life: scientists, doctors, nurses, housewives, office workers, teachers, etc.

Aside from the orchestra, the musical life in the city flourished and grew to what was probably the highest percentage in the country for cities with equivalent population. Although I was a well-trained cellist with an excellent musical background, I had had no specific training in conducting. Nor had I ever expected or particularly wanted it. But, in spite of the many besetting problems, I acquired confidence in myself; and through what others were kind enough to call my enthusiasm and guidance, the orchestra thrived. Two examples of the problems I encountered in an uncharted field: Shortly before the second concert, a bassoonist left town. I then had to rearrange the score so that another instrument could play the part. At the third concert, both bassoonists were gone, and two scores needed to be rearranged.

World-famous artists have played with the Oak Ridge Symphony, including Isaac Stern and accompanist Alexander Zakin, Yalta Menuhin, Albert Spalding, Lili Kraus, Grainger and others. Many members of the orchestra (H. Pomerance, the Silvermans, Jacinta Howard, I and others later) played in the Knoxville Symphony Orchestra, and carried the extra load of attending rehearsals in both cities. Further, with the unusually high amount of talent in Oak Ridge, there was enough to have an exceptionally fine chorus, chamber music groups, etc. A series of Sunday night "Coffee Concerts" was started where varied chamber programs were given free to the public by vocalists, piano soloists, quartet players and the like—all amateurs.

The coming of world-renowned musicians to Oak Ridge did more than enrich our listening. In 1980, I wrote down my recollection of one long-ago visit:

Isaac Stern was one of the great artists who performed with the Oak Ridge Symphony Orchestra. The first time was on February 7, 1948—a Saturday night. Isaac and his long-time accompanist, Alexander Zakin, were to leave Monday morning. This gave them a "free" Sunday to rehearse for their next engagement. As luck would have it, our Steinway Grand was in tune, and we invited them to practice at our house. They arrived about 1 P.M., changed into comfortable slacks and T-shirts and went right to work. Our Steinway never sounded so grand.

As the glorious sound of their music poured out of the windows, crowds gathered on the street and overflowed to the boardwalk next to our house. There were enough listeners outside to fill a concert hall.

It was soon evident that rehearsing was no easy task—it required the stamina of a stevedore; and it struck me that Isaac and Alexander were going to need plenty of nourishment. On hand were a bag of potatoes, some eggs and a picnic ham, thanks to a GI sitter who had given me some food stamps. Lowly fare for internationally renown artists; but in true Oak Ridge style, it would have to do.

However, by late afternoon, the house was filled with orchestra friends who had tiptoed in and were quietly and raptly listening and occupying all the seating and floor space. So far, our supper "en famille" had expanded to about thirty guests. Still more were phoning, and I urged them to come—with extra food. By the time the practice session was over, the dining table was loaded with salads, casseroles and desserts galore. Everything but extra meat!

Isaac could make himself at home anywhere in the world—his geniality, humor and charm are legendary. In no time, he seemed part of our family. He followed me into the kitchen to lend a helping hand and found me staring hopelessly at that ham, which appeared to be shrinking before my eyes.

"What's the trouble, little mama?" he asked. "Can I help?"

I wailed *sotto voce*, "Do I need help! Only to stretch this puny ham to feed forty people."

He surveyed it thoughtfully and pronounced, "No problem, at all. Just hand me a sharp knife."

I shall never forget the spectacle of Isaac Stern, wrapped in a huge apron, brandishing the knife and carving—or rather shaving—that ham into paper-thin slices with the finesse of a master chef. It almost equalled his musical genius. Then in a conspiratorial tone, he whispered that a discreet word passed to specific friends to go easy or "bypass" the meat would make it go even further. The plot worked. Everybody was fed, and I still marvel that there was enough meat left over for a tasty sandwich the next day!

A woman who made her living teaching music was delighted with what she found when she came to Oak Ridge. Alice Lyman gave this account of her introduction to Oak Ridge as she remembered it:

> Oak Ridge has always been one continuous series of exciting events for me ever since June, 1944. I had been studying, playing, and teaching in New York City and its environs since 1929. In 1944, I was teaching vocal and instrumental music in an elementary school on Long Island, and had an organist and choir director's position in Brooklyn. Now, New York City has a way of getting under one's skin, and I never dreamed of working anywhere else. But a visit to my brother and his family in Raleigh, North Carolina, that summer changed my life completely.
>
> While in Raleigh, I received a telegram from Superintendent A. H. Blankenship asking me to come to Duke University in Durham for an interview concerning a teaching position in Oak Ridge, Tennessee. Fortunately, my brother, who had been with the North Carolina Power and Light Company for a number of years, was familiar with the TVA. He had heard more about Oak Ridge than I had, and he encouraged me to look into the matter.
>
> The minute I met Dr. B., as we all got to call him, I knew I wanted to work with him. He had the most contagious smile I have ever seen, and he gave me the most direct and satisfying answers I have ever heard.
>
> I asked him, "What are they doing over there in Oak Ridge?"
>
> And he replied, "If I knew, I'm under oath not to tell you; but, honestly, I don't know."
>
> Well, I asked him what he wanted me to do over there. Just as directly, he answered, "I want to put you into Elm Grove Elementary School. I want you to teach music in grades four through eight, and do everything possible in instrumental music—despite our limited equipment. We are a closed city;

the Army is in charge. We have to do without many things, but our spirits are high and we want you to teach them that."

When I went back to New York City, I resigned my two jobs. In August, I packed my wardrobe trunk and a big wooden box of music and books and boarded the Southern Railway train for Knoxville. The day coach, which we rode all night, was overcrowded with both civilians and soldiers; but everyone was cheerful and friendly. We took turns sitting down and standing up and working our way up and down the aisles and sitting in soldiers' laps.

We arrived in Knoxville in the morning, and, at the station information desk, I found two other teachers going to Oak Ridge. We explored Gay Street together and had lunch at Weaver's Cafe. In midafternoon, we caught an Army bus to Oak Ridge. We entered the city by way of Elza Gate, where we were processed and then deposited in our own prospective abodes. Mine was W-5, a women's dormitory called Carlisle Hall. A group of us from the dormitory ate supper at the cafeteria on Central Avenue, where the Village Restaurant is now, and explored Townsite—now called Jackson Square. We arrived at the Ridge Recreation Hall—Oak Ridge Library and cafe at that time—in time for a community sing with Gladys Carringer providing the swinging piano music, and oh, was she ever good!

What impressed me most about Oak Ridge at night were all the electric lights. It was bright as daytime and free buses were traveling in every direction. The dust in the street had to be at least two inches deep. The week of Teachers' Workshop at Elm Grove School was a delightful experience with Principal Paul Anthony and a grand staff of teachers.

Friday noon, when I had gotten my music room beautifully arranged with musical pictures and charts waiting for my little charges on Monday morning, Mr. Anthony came in and leaned against the door. He told me, apologetically, that school enrollment would be much greater by Monday morning, and that I would have to move my music room out into one of the four portables behind the schoolhouse.

Now, a portable is a one-room job with a potbellied stove right in the middle of it. But I had a fairly good piano and plenty of blackboard and bulletin space, so I was in pretty good shape. Over the weekend it began to rain—forty days and forty nights. I was prepared with red rubber boots, and I remember that between classes I picked up clods of mud which had fallen off the children's shoes and plopped them into the wastebasket. I said to the principal, "Does it rain down here all the time?"

He said, "I can remember one day last year that it did not rain."

The talent and enthusiasm I encountered every day in my students was an endless joy. They loved to sing and dance, try any musical instrument we could find, and all the instruments that we had were those that had been brought to Oak Ridge by the students themselves from their former home-towns. At school, I worked with any child who had an instrument, teaching him how to play it. We finally got fifteen children together to make a small band—plus a young girl who played the piano. We had dancing classes for the seventh and eighth grades. The principal would come into the gymnasium and make the boys dance with the girls. Sometimes they didn't want to, but he'd say, "You have to do that, now. The girls are not going to bite you." The orchestra got so it could play little waltzes and two-steps for the children to dance to.

The quality of education was high. The schools had been going since December '43, so when I came they were already set up. Dr. Blankenship and the teachers (not the Army) set up the curriculum. I had quite a lot of freedom. I had brought a lot of things with me from previous situations—music and picture books. Dr. Blankenship encouraged us to do all we wanted with the children. The ten schools were situated all over the city, so Elm Grove did not have a cross section.

In addition, there was the black school, where they had only black teachers. I was used to segregation in Alabama, so it seemed natural in Oak Ridge. However, when I got my band going at Jefferson Junior High, we went over to the black school to give an assembly program. The different schools swapped programs. The music teachers—including the blacks—would get together for workshops. So we knew what was going on in all the schools. I made a chorus in each homeroom from the fourth grade through the eighth, and put them together for special occasions. I remember a May Day: We stayed out of doors all day with singing, dancing and the band playing.

The woman before me had started a marching band, because they had so many parades in Oak Ridge. They'd have a Thanksgiving Day parade, a Christmastime parade, Veteran's Day, Fourth of July, Fire Prevention Week—you name it! It didn't need much of an excuse to have a parade to keep up the morale of the town!

I had never been in such a city with such an active musical life—especially for its size. I had been brought up where we had one elementary school and one high school. But Oak Ridge was like a bunch of little towns with each one having its own school. There were so many people here and so many things going on.

And there were the three shifts; there was just a difference in the way the town lived. It was going twenty-four hours a day in eight-hour shifts. So there was activity going on twenty-four hours a day. The lights were on all night—all night long.

Oak Ridge was a delightful town to me. There was always plenty to do in the city. I got involved immediately in musical life, and a Square Dance Society among other activities. And there were always interesting things to read in the library. But I enjoyed the people more than anything else.

The Feldmans also enjoyed the abundant music of Oak Ridge. Here is what Cy had to say:

> We're both very fond of music, although we don't play any instrument well enough to let anybody hear us. This do-it-yourself city in every regard included the orchestra and other musical events. So we did civilian jobs along those lines and had a feeling of sharing in it, which was important to us. [2]

---

[2]None of the cultural activities depended on patronage by a power structure or wealthy contributors.

We have people come here from the outside, and when we tell them what's available in a city of 30,000 today, they can't believe it. Of course, it's due to the history of Oak Ridge and the high average level of education, etc. of the people. Both things have helped.

I had written to Margaret that possibly only in church could you find a cross section of Oak Ridge society, and, indeed, the need for religion cut through the social strata of Oak Ridge from its start. Here is what some of the early comers had to say about it.

Charmian and Waldo Cohn: There were no organized religious institutions in the beginning, but various denominations met at different times at the Chapel on the Hill. A little later, some denominations, due to the need for more space, held services at assorted places such as movie houses and schoolrooms. Some had held the hope for some kind of unified religion for those who felt the need. This idea died early in 1944. Today Oak Ridge abounds in religious institutions of just about every denomination. Some of the buildings are modest and others as elaborate as one finds in any other city of comparable size.

Kathryn Cantrell: Oak Ridge was a full life. It was frontier. It was construction camp. It was inhibited adventure. One would wonder that religion would ever find a place here. But it did.

For, right at first, the three Army-type chapels that were built were used. In fact, the request for space much exceeded the space that was available. So arrangements were made for religious groups to hold their meetings in classrooms of the schools, in school auditoriums, in theaters, and in the Ridge Recreation Hall. But by the early 1950's, churches had begun to dot the landscape. St. Mary's Catholic Church had built their school, and used the gymnasium for worship services. It is amazing to think that these young families, who could not yet buy their own home, would commit themselves to the responsibilities that were necessary to make these attractive, functional structures possible for their and succeeding generations' religious nurture. They gave tangible evidence of their intent to make this a permanent community.

Religion was pervasive in Oak Ridge, as it was in most places. Security was pervasive there, too, which it was not elsewhere, and it was the latter that made our town unique. Ruth Carey told of an instance in which the two elements met. It was also a moment when her characterization of life in Oak Ridge—"we had a ball"—turned out to be matzo balls—many, many matzo balls:

They had a Passover seder for the Jewish people here, and there was a woman, who was about thirty-five and to me a very authoritarian figure. She told me, "You are in charge of the Matzo Ball Committee." I had never made a matzo ball in my life and I didn't know how to!

We had about three hundred at the seder and it started with a security lecture from someone in the Army. "It's OK to write your mother that you went to a seder, but don't tell her how many people were there," he said. The reason was that if someone wanted to figure out how many people were in Oak Ridge, he could take the Jewish population of the United States as a certain part of the total and then figure out how many people there were in Oak Ridge altogether.

I went to a telephone booth ahead of time and called my aunt in Knoxville and asked, "How do you make matzo balls?"

"Well," she said, "you take an egg and a half-cup of matzo meal . . . "

So I went to a place in Oak Terrace that had great big pots like those that you see in cartoons where the cannibals are boiling a missionary, and got a pot and we made the soup in that. We had gotten our supplies from a Jewish national charity that was trying to help soldiers, so we had boxes and boxes of matzo meal. I had on an evening dress, but I took thousands of eggs and the meal and dumped them in a great big bowl and another woman and I stood there and rolled those matzo balls. I didn't know what I was doing, but they were marvelous! Which all goes to show that if you don't know that you don't know how to do something, you can usually do it.

Letter XXIV

Oak Ridge, Tenn.
May 20, 1948

Dear Margaret,

Connie is a month old today, and I must say Oak Ridge babies are a success. They get you out of bed the day after a baby is born and send you home a week later feeling practically normal. The following week I started driving the car, and made my debut at a morning "Coffee Klatch."

Grandmother season has started again, and tomorrow Mother and I are going to a tea where other grandmas will be. This is another new fashionable practice. It is a pleasant shock to see so many gray-haired ladies about all of a sudden.

No doubt you saw Stephen White's article in the Herald Tribune, May 19.[1] He did a beautiful job on reporting faithfully what he learned here. The situation is really acute and cannot be overestimated. Very few of the scientists feel they can continue working under such conditions. The worst part of it all was that an attempt was made by most of the top men and some of the scientists in key positions to keep the investigation hush-hush. In fact, there was a case at Brookhaven, and the guy was sent to Oak Ridge for his trial so it would not leak out.

The Knoxville papers have made the Herald Tribune story headline news for two days and very good coverage. This publicity is the first ray of hope that something will be done to stop the inquisitions.

Last night some of our friends were returning from Knoxville about 1:30 A.M. and were stopped at the gate and told they were not permitted to enter. They protested that they were residents and wanted to go home to bed. The guards told them there was a "state of emergency" and they weren't even allowed to use the phone. There was a line of cars inside and outside the gate

---

[1] See pages 189-90.

and all were kept waiting for thirty-five minutes and then permitted on their way. We understand this happens frequently. No explanations given.

You know Oak Ridge is reputed to be the safest city in the country. They are also determined to be the cleanest. Right now is the "Clean-up Campaign." All the children brought questionnaires home from school. There were questions about garbage, yards and also "Have you washed your walls?" "Have you painted your porch?" "Have you cleaned your closets?"

And speaking of schools, I recently discovered that spanking children for not doing homework and other disciplinary reasons is condoned here—and we are supposed to have one of the most progressive school systems! Maybe I am out of date.

There is more and more talk of making this a "normal" town, the possibility of eliminating the gates, etc. Almost everyone one speaks to is against it for various reasons. Some feel it is thoroughly impractical, others want it to remain "exclusive," some feel that since we might have to be a part of Anderson County, we would inherit their dirty political machine, too. Then there is the question of houses. Rumor has it that they will be put up for sale with the occupants having first option to buy. Well, these houses are cute and convenient in many ways, but so flimsy they are in constant need of repair, and no one wants to be forced to buy one.[2] Then there are taxes. Who wants to pay for the support of the town, or be bothered with buying coal, paying the carpenter, plumber, electrician? And who wants all the strangers coming around here to picnic? There are plenty of them as is.

This week will be the last issue of the Oak Ridge Journal. A daily newspaper is starting in June. It will be interesting to see the type of local paper we have here. At the rate people are leaving, wonder who will be left to read it.

We, too, are considering moving into Knoxville. Up to now, Dick has been able to do pure research at the Lab, but very soon his work will be limited to certain fields. He doesn't feel he wants to be restricted or do any research connected with military problems, and he also reacts unfavorably to the dismal atmosphere at the Lab. I will let you know as soon as we are more certain.

I have attended several meetings of the committee studying Homemaker Service for the Family Service Bureau. Our principal hope is to get the AEC to arrange to have regular paid Homemakers on the staff and that they will be permitted to live here on that basis. There is so much red tape that I wonder if it will ever amount to anything. Anyway, we have worked for months and the report is about ready to be handed in.

Connie has just reminded me that I'm writing on her time. Dick sends regards and says to thank Gregory for the reprints.

As ever,
[sig] Thelma

---

[2]These so-called cute, flimsy cemesto houses have proved to be sturdy and durable beyond all expectation-T.P., 1980

New York City
June 5, 1948

Dear Thelma,

I am a fine correspondent not even to have written you about the baby's birth, or the news of which we were very glad. (Fine sentence, you can see the state I am in . . . end of term, too many meetings, papers, etc.) Your last letter interested me specially in the stuff about people's being afraid of the penalties of being a real town. I don't believe we can possibly have too much data on this, as it is a real danger in our society at present. So any more you have.[3] I admire your energy so soon after the baby's birth.

We plan a staggered summer. Gregory is in the country now for a couple of weeks, then back for a month of work, then up to the country with Cathy. I go to Europe the 19th of July for six weeks work on the International Conference on Mental Health, back early in September. It all does really get used, although sometimes in ways hard to document. Regards to Dick from both of us.

Yours,
[sig] Margaret

Chairmian and Waldo Cohn had some interesting views on how Oak Ridge work, housing, social life and the attachments people formed changed over the years. From their interview:

The men worked six long days a week, were totally absorbed by their work, and were glad to have a restful evening at home or to tackle household jobs.

When the war ended, there was an exodus of about 45,000 people—including scientists and construction workers. Some returned to their former jobs, and others were terminated, and the population leveled off to 30,000. It has remained so up to the present.

Scientists, engineers, administrators and a few high Army personnel had top priority on housing. Exceptions to the general rule of assignment were made for administrators and upper-echelon Army men. A top Army man, with no or few children, could have one of the choice houses in a "cream" neighborhood—usually an F on top of the ridge.

Social life was compartmentalized. Scientists formed a large group and were on top of the scale, except for the few high Army men. There was hardly any social interaction between these two groups. However, the Army wives (top level) considered themselves the elite.

On a descending scale were educators, bankers, businessmen, etc., and at the lower end were mechanics, maintenance workers, shop workers and unskilled laborers, few of whom had real houses in the town, lived in Hutments or outside, or in one of the eighty-three huge dormitories or barracks.

---

[3]This is in answer to my query to Margaret if I was sending the proper material.

In the '60s or '70s, the '43 Club was started, made up of a cross section of the city. Anybody who had arrived in 1943 was eligible to join, provided they were still residing here—the Oak Ridge equivalent of the DAR. There are about a hundred who meet twice a year; no purpose except to reminisce. In the beginning, which was 1943, no one even thought of such a club.

(To get their ideas of Oak Ridge in 1980, I asked the Cohns: "In what ways has it 'normalized', and in what ways is it still unique?"—*T.P.*)

Physically, many residents bought the homes in which they had been living when the Atomic Energy Commission put them up for sale at a ridiculously low cost after the city was "opened up" in the 1950s. These homes now are almost beyond recognition. At first, people got rid of the colors the Army had allotted. Then siding was added, extra rooms built and basements finished for guest rooms or family living. Some covered the old cemesto on the outside with wood and/or brick, and added carports. Gardens abound. These changes have so enhanced the houses that they can vie with homes found in attractive neighborhoods in any other city.

Others decided to build their own homes, and new neighborhoods expanded the city in all directions. Most of the new houses are elegant and expansive, as well as expensive. There is now the usual commercialization with neon lights, fast food restaurants and motels that one sees all over this country.

But from a cultural view, Oak Ridge is still unique. What other city of its size has as great a concentration of some of the best scientists in the country— even attracting many from other countries? Where are such close-knit friendships bonded together from their common war experience?

What other city of its size sustains an excellent orchestra, Community Theater, fine Ballet Company, Art Center, Civic Center, Museum of Atomic Energy, choirs and choruses? All of these groups have wide community participation and are mostly self-supporting. There are strongly supported political groups and all kinds of interest groups.

Oak Ridge is one of the main centers of Recording for the Blind, housed in a fine building with excellent equipment and many volunteer readers in several specialties. There is, too, an unusual and original Children's Museum. Oak Ridge scientists are probably among the most widely traveled—exchanging or gaining scientific information from all over the world. People come and go, but the population remains stable at about thirty thousand.

("Why did so many of the scientists elect to remain in Oak Ridge?"—T. P.)

Many had invitations to work at some of our most prestigious universities or institutions. (Waldo had a request from Harvard.) Those who continued to stay on felt that the scientific work in Oak Ridge was more interesting than the war work. Many things and much research were needed for the benefit of the future. They enjoyed the climate, the life and other benefits—although regretting many of the aspects of becoming a "normal" city. Salaries are still better than the average university, particularly those in the South. They still enjoy the "easy" and informal social life.

Cy and Rose Feldman had similar feelings about living in Oak Ridge. He said:

> At the end of the war, many scientists left—some to go back to jobs or to take other jobs. But we stayed on. I was doing the kind of work I liked and it looked as if it would continue indefinitely. It was a matter of "bird in hand," I suppose. I liked living in Oak Ridge. I had never lived in a place outside of a big city; but, perforce, we had been living here for several years, and I got the exposure I might not have had if I had automatically assumed that you had to live in a big city. We had enough experience by then and I was pretty well situated.
>
> We also got involved, even by then, in community activities to an extent which we probably would not have done had we been in a big city.

Rose added:

> We hadn't put roots down in Washington, where we had lived just a few months. We hadn't really made many friends, except a few temporary ones. We had made friends here on all levels. We loved the outdoors. We loved the Smokies. And we loved the informality of life here.

Bettie Levy compared the early and present (1980) days in Oak Ridge and told of her delight in it as a place to live:

> Until I moved to Oak Ridge, I'd had little experience with the passes and guards. Since the secrecy was no problem to me, it didn't bother me. For one thing, I was young and it was just great for Henri to pick me up at the gate. Then when I moved to Oak Ridge, it was rather nice. We had a closed community. We never had to lock up because the whole town was guarded. It was like being in a very well-preserved private place.
>
> You know that Oak Ridge citizens fought having it made into an open town: "Now my mother-in-law can visit without having to give prior notice!" To me it didn't matter one way or the other. It was very, very pleasant. I enjoyed all the privileges of being in a closed city, because we certainly had all the privileges and no responsibility. The guards cooperated with us 110 percent. It was extremely nice to live in this lovely community.
>
> The famous Boston firm of architects that laid out the city—with its winding paths—destroyed a minimum of trees and foliage and sort of kept to the terrain. It is a shame that we didn't keep up with those various master plans. I think the turnpike is deteriorating today with all those fast food places.
>
> When Union Carbide took over running the Lab, many people started to

leave. Union Carbide was considered to have a very old-fashioned, backward commercial factory-type policy. Henri received some nice offers at various places to go back to academic life. But by that time I had fallen in love with East Tennessee and its four equal seasons and the beauty of the countryside. Coming from Southern California where everything is desert like, I felt the mountains sort of made up for the sea. I still miss the ocean, but I think this is God's country.

I said, "How do you feel about your job? Do you want the very best possible job or does the climate and terrain make a difference?"

He decided that—looking at the totality—he would try Union Carbide. I think the big advantage is that we had Alvin Weinberg as the director of the Lab, and he taught some sense about it, and it turned out to be a very good company to work for. Henri kept on having offers to go elsewhere, but by that time we were completely entrenched in Oak Ridge.

We are in a very beautiful part of the city. Meadow Road is right in the old part of town where they didn't bulldoze all the trees away. We have a greenbelt right behind us. You just go right down the hill and there you are in Jackson Square, the Playhouse, and it is so easy to get everywhere. I don't think we would move for anything now.

You know what is unique about Oak Ridge—not unique—but rather rare in this country? It is a college town without a college. It has the advantages of being a small college town. While it has the vestiges of having been a company town, it has the nice things that go along with that—well-laid-out streets, and the advantages of the arts with an unusually high proportion of educated people who appreciate the arts. I think it is way ahead of the average town in the United States with around 25,000 to 30,000 population. In a college town you have all these cliques and the Town and Gown, but Oak Ridge escapes some of that because of having not only a big industry but smaller industries also. Now we are even getting a small community college here. Roane State is working toward having a branch here.

The biggest problem today, in my opinion, is the lack of public transportation here. In the early days, transportation was provided partly because of gas rationing (and no new automobiles were being built during the war). It was subsidized by the government and never paid for itself. There is not any real reason why public transportation should pay for itself completely—especially if you have a city like Oak Ridge, which is so many miles long. We should consider it, like some of the other public utilities, as something the state helps provide. But that is a philosophy this country has to come to. In other countries, transportation systems are just part of the town planning. We have not come to that in the United States yet.

An experience I remember with a local person was when I was riding the bus to visit friends soon after the war. The driver was pointing out places and saying, "I used to go squirrel hunting there, and over there is where my parents' farm was. When I got back from the war and saw this long town, it was quite a shock. The whole city grew up where we had our farm land."

Another thing is that TVA had to relocate families when they built the dams. Some of these same people had to be relocated again, later, when the

Manhattan District came along. The story I heard from them was that they sure liked the way TVA relocated them better than the way the Manhattan District handled them. It was kind of rough. And yet, you know, the East Tennessee natives are just a real hardy breed. They have lived through all these upheavals and have come out with their sanity. Some of them lost a great deal, and I feel that even when you get government compensation, it doesn't make up for a farm that has been in your family for generations. But, after all, that was quite a war we fought.

When they opened the gates [on March 19, 1949] and had the big celebration, we sat on the porch of our little apartment on Wade Lane listening to all the excitement. Janny was a tiny infant, and I was just home and didn't want to go anywhere. We thought that it was nice that they were opening up the city, because that is the right thing to do when you live in a democracy. I mean, we had all those privileges because it was required. We had them longer than we should have, and it was time to give them up.

As Bette commented on the hardiness of the East Tennessee natives and of the upheavals that were forced on many of them, the secrecy in Oak Ridge also spawned tales by them of humor as well as terror. Writing in *The Antioch Review*, Clifford Seeber, who grew up in the Tennessee Valley, told of such incidents in an article, "Acorns to Atoms."[4] The following are some excerpts:

What's Cooking?

The late President Roosevelt's fetish of "nothing to fear but fear itself" applies to the native attitude toward all the hush-hush secrecy of Oak Ridge. The only mystery to the natives was why it was a mystery. They couldn't see why the Government didn't just announce what it was trying to do and do it, without all the fuss and feathers.

Although East Tennesseans are still odds-on favorites to find out more about where a stranger comes from, what he came for, and where he's going than any other group of people in the world, including the former German Gestapo and the present F.B.I.—they still maintain they are not nosy. They are, by and large, as taciturn in revealing information as they are persistent in acquiring it. But they just hate to be kept in the dark.

As soon as the project started, they began trying to figure it out. One local Sherlock Holmes, as early as 1943, had his theory: "It's a device for splitting the atom. Exactly how it works, I can't say, but it goes something like this— you set a little gadget here, press a button, and say 'git Adolph,' and everything around Berlin just blows up."

But the natives were not the only ones who were curious. One lady tourist spent several days trying to unravel the mystery. Her curiosity was first aroused when she breezed into a newspaper office and asked, "What are they making at this Oak Ridge Project down there?"

---

[4]From "A Grass Roots History of Oak Ridge," *The Antioch Review*, vol. XII, September 1952.

The editor replied, "I don't know."

"Well," she demanded, "who does know?"

Again he pleaded ignorance.

She exploded indignantly: "What right has the Government got to take the taxpayers' money and not tell people what it is being used for? Part of my tax money is going into that plant, and I'm going to find out what they are making." She stormed out like old Hudibras. What success she had in her venture is still unknown.

So far as is known, however, only one native took the secret seriously enough to quit his job in protest. "You're wasting too much money down here," the employee declared. His foreman pointed out that since he didn't know what was being made he couldn't know that the money was being wasted. "I don't care what it is," he declared, "from the money they are spending to make it, I know it would be cheaper for the Government to buy it already made. . ."

All in all, the mystery of Oak Ridge provided a lot of fun for curious natives—and a fourteen-carat headache for top-ranking project officials. . .

East Tennesseans, like the world over, were naturally stunned by the Hiroshima episode. But they were not, and are not yet, able to grasp the full significance of "atomic energy. . ."

For one thing, a number of highly vocal New Deal critics were silenced. It also took the wind out of the sails of party-conscious Republicans . . .

Now that the intriguing secret was revealed, they began to view Oak Ridge from a different perspective. They became suddenly aware that in three years a city had grown from nothing to the fifth-largest in Tennessee. . .

No one was able to put into words his conception of the product itself. There were fragments of philosophy here and there; "the beginning of the end of time"; "a discovery that will destroy civilization." But for the most part, local philosophers, when asked to comment, just shook their heads and said nothing. One minister, after urging his flock, gave this version; whether he clarified the issue or muddied the water, no one seemed to know:

For over five thousand years, now, ever since Adam and Eve first started eating apples that growed on the tree of knowledge, man has been trying to figure out what makes this old universe tick. He has explored the bowels of the earth, the depths of the sea, and has sailed like a bird through the sky. But he ain't never found the secret in none of these places. Then he got out his microscope and his telescope and he has looked down and he's looked up, but he ain't never seen nothing that would give him the answer. Lately he has been tinkering with electricity and sound waves and radar, but in these he ain't got more than a few hints. He ain't found out the secret.

But now he has gone and done it! In this here atom-splitting business he has discovered the secret of the universe. He knows now the stuff that the earth and man is made of. The only thing he don't know now, is what he is going to do with what he does know.

The parson paused and the audience was still. Then he concluded his sermon: "You all asked me to preach on this new atomic power, and I've tried to do so. You want to know what we can do about this power so's it won't destroy us. Now they's only one thing I know of that we can do, and that is this——" He paused and the audience craned its neck to hear the answer.

He opened his mouth, but no words came. It was as if he had been struck dumb. He tried again, but still no words. Then he sank to one knee, lowered his head, and said simply, "Let us pray."

But if the culture, the friendships and informality, and the natural beauty of Oak Ridge were praised by people like the Pomerances, Feldmans and Levys as making it a good place to live—it was also a city that had had its times of trouble.

On August 1, 1946, President Truman signed the Atomic Energy Act of 1946, establishing the Atomic Energy Commission to set and guide the country's policy on atomic energy. The legislation was better known as the McMahon Act after Senator Brien McMahon of Connecticut, the first chairman of the Senate-House Joint Atomic Energy Committee.

David E. Lilienthal, former chairman of TVA, was named to head the five-man group.

Though the AEC officially took over from the Manhattan Project January 1, 1947, Lilienthal and the other commissioners were not to take office until April 9 of that year. During the Senate hearings on this issue, which would involve the transfer of more land than the state of Rhode Island and more material and equipment than could be stored in the Empire State Building, Lilienthal said: "I believe in—and I conceive the Constitution of the United States to rest upon, as does religion—the fundamental proposition of the integrity of the individual; and that all Government and private institutions must be designed to promote and protect and defend the integrity and the dignity of the individual . . . "

But between such idealistic theory and bureaucratic practice, a vast chasm developed. Herbert Pomerance said:

The McMahon Act that set up the AEC required an FBI investigation of everyone. And the FBI would send the information to the AEC with a disclaimer that "we don't evaluate this information, this is only what we turned up." And the AEC didn't go to the trouble of evaluating.

As a result, there were a lot of nasty security hearings based on hearsay that an FBI man recorded and sent in. The security hearings were held in various places. I know at least part of them were held in Tulsa, Oklahoma, because a man had married a girl from Tulsa and the information against him was really information against her. There was an appeal, and he did have a lawyer for it.

The quality of the information that the appeal board had to listen to at these hearings was so terrible that John Swartout, who was on some of the boards (and later was deputy director at the Lab), talked to a Chemical Society meeting about the poor quality of the information served up.

But, meanwhile, the way they handled the people was terrible. One young fellow was served his notice at suppertime and told to turn in his badge. As a result of that, Kay Way[5] invited the *Herald Tribune* to send a reporter down here. He came down and spent three days and wrote things up, using quotes from letters like "among the things you may have left behind [at an address before coming to Oak Ridge] may have been copies of the New Masses."

Or they would ask the landlady:

"Did he have any Communist literature?"

"I don't remember."

"Did he leave the New Masses?"

"Maybe he did."

---

[5]Dr. Kay Way was the instigator of the *Herald Tribune* stories referred to on page 181. The reporter was Stephen White of the *Herald Tribune*.

Letter XXV

Dear Margaret,

Upon reading the papers shortly after our lunch appointment, I realized why you had to break it. Thousands of people like me who had never met Ruth Benedict except through her writings felt her death to be almost a personal loss, so I can imagine what it has meant to you.

As for my not writing up to now, well, the Knoxville Story is very different from the Oak Ridge one. I had quite forgotten that we were living in a completely different world there. I wonder if we would have had to make as much of an adjustment had we moved back to New York.

There were many things about Oak Ridge that I wanted to tell you. For several weeks after the news broke about "opening" the city, I tried to get the reactions of various types of people and here is a condensed result.

—Wife of a Lab director, "Damn their hides!"

—Wife of an AEC official, "Can't take this city anymore. We're moving to Washington."

—Physicist's wife, "Definitely against it! Who wants to be like East Tennessee? It will be bad economically and never will be normal whatever they do. Think of the burglary and lack of safety."

—Housewife and ex-schoolteacher, "I think it's terrible! No safety from burglary. Have to lock our doors. People think we make lots of money here, so will be more of a tendency to thieve. Don't think industry will ever develop here."

—Wives of several scientists, "Maybe we'll have some nice hotels or tearooms, but don't think much of the idea. Who wants to be stuck with these houses if the Government decides to move the plant? Will be like any East

191

Tennessee town. Level of schools will be lower. Oak Ridge will be overrun with tourists and curiosity seekers. This town was built for scientists, and businesses were brought in to serve them. Industry will never grow. Can't see manufacture or industry—not enough permanency for that. Think of all the thieving. Our children won't be safe. We'll have to lock our doors. The place will be full of motor courts. Have to find the key to the house and have to lock our cars. Maybe we'll have some better restaurants, better hotels, better shops, better club buildings."

—Most prominent remarks from various people including some scientists, doctor's wife, business people: Worry about tourists and hope there will be some control over them. Residents may still need passes. Some don't mind the idea, didn't object to tourists, but concerned about the whole question of housing. Willing to give it a try, but skeptical about Oak Ridge ever being normal—too much confusion about everything. Doctor's wife: "The hospital will be open to nearby towns that have no adequate medical care."

Almost everyone mentions burglary. All business people in favor. Will have competition and free enterprise, business from nearby towns. Local residents in favor of having easier contact with nearby friends. All wondering—many worried about question of renting or buying houses or property. Can outsiders come in and buy or build? Will our houses be sold over our heads? Some ready to buy houses as soon as for sale. Feel houses will be very cheap. Some feel Oak Ridge is here to stay and it will be a golden opportunity for industry. Most oft-heard remark—Just like any East Tennessee town. Lots of resentment over not being consulted and not having any voice as to the type of government to have.

Well, that was the gist of things. On top of it, the private newspaper that started as a daily last July collapsed after a few weeks, and as someone said, "That was the final degradation of Oak Ridge." There is still no source of local news except the radio, and rumors were thicker than usual. Incidentally, the Oak Ridge radio station tried to meet the deficiency, and their most popular program was a fifteen minutes twice daily of classified ads. We got rid of several household items that way before we moved.

Now that the time is approaching for the gates to be opened—and, by the way, two or three gates near the plants will be closed completely to the public—our friends are interested in our struggles in the wide world. What we pay for coal. How we order it. They are aghast at our having to pay for some plumbing and carpentering. What does our electric bill come to? In fact, all the problems of maintenance are as much a mystery to them as they were to us. Many people want to leave Oak Ridge and yet shrink at the thought of another way of life.

There are things that I will always remember as being indigenous only to Oak Ridge. Principally, the youngness of it—the young people—the city bursting with little children, overrun by pet dogs, the informality—the baby-sitting movements for almost everything including meetings, illness, booths for leaving children while voting, freedom from household responsibilities, the picnics for almost every occasion. Particularly the last one at Big Ridge where there was every conceivable device set up for babies, bassinets, car beds, playpens, strollers, collapsible carriages, blankets, the mothers form-ing groups to take turns watching babies while parents went swimming, walking, or just mingling with friends. The mutualness of people's lives made the patterns seem very simple. One woman expressed the following senti-ment which I believe is generally felt, "Well, the change was inevitable. We have to recognize that we must stand on our own two feet now. The honey-moon is over. It was nice while it lasted."

And so the Oak Ridge story has come to the end of the chapter. I feel that I could have done better—so many things I should have said, and perhaps many I shouldn't have said. It leaves me feeling unsatisfied, and writing about Oak Ridge is one purpose of my existence which I shall miss a great deal.

Living in Knoxville for me has become a grim determination to end the Civil War. Southern hospitality is strictly for the South, and being a Yankee, plus a New Yorker, has at least two points against me. I was in a bake shop today and a man rushed in for breads. He talked like a Northerner, and I barely restrained myself from saying, "You speak English!" I had the feeling I was in a foreign country and here was a "lantzman."

In addition to the Southern psychology, there is the hillbilly mentality. Everybody is so polite, so concerned about you and full of promises, but nothing gets done. You just learn to wait until they get around to you. The social functions are very "hatty and glovey" and full of receiving lines, and the social codes are so strict and conventional that I always wind up feeling like a gawky schoolgirl. This applies not only to life centered about the University, to which all local people refer as the "Hill," but also most outside affairs.[1]

After hunting desperately for several weeks for decent household help, I finally acquired dear Mrs.———, who is unadulterated hillbilly. Erskine Caldwell has misled me about the po' whites. She's a God-lovin' woman, has a passion for waxing floors "'cause hit takes the cricks outa muh neck." She uses Bruton Scotch snuff. She composes and sings religious songs over the radio and all children are "eyngels" from Heav'n. She brings her youngest, out of five, to work, providing a much-needed playmate for Irene. Two of the girls sit for us and her boy is coming to "do up" our yard, and we're all beginning to talk like her, praise the Lord! They live in a little shack and whenever I call her on the phone, someone answers "Mrs.———'s residence."

Bless muh soul, if hit ain't 1:00! Gotta say muh prayers and git to bed. Hallelujah!

[sig] Thelma

---

[1]The move to Knoxville meant as much of an adjustment as it had been from New York to Oak Ridge. But, gradually, my Yankee prejudices gave way to an understanding, respect and affecton towards the differences in my adopted city. Once, on our annual trip to New York, we were caught in heavy trafic entering the city. A passenger in a car parallel to ours—upon seeing our license plates—called out scathingly, "Here come the Hillbillies!" With pride, I yelled back, "You all come see us!" It struck me then that New York was no longer "home," but a nice place to visit.

An era had ended for us with our move from Oak Ridge, bringing with it the bittersweet mixture of sadness and exhilaration at the coming challenges. Others had felt similar mixed emotions at the end of the war when they learned of the cost in lives that their work had taken to bring it about. From the perspective of 1980, Cy Feldman looked back on those days and the history written in them:

> At that time and for several years before that, the Marines and the Army in the Western Pacific were losing thousands of men. The fighting was desperate on those islands; and although they were slowly pushing the Japanese back to Japan, they were going to have to invade Japan eventually. Judging by the casualties on Okinawa and Guadalcanal and all the rest of the islands, they were expecting something like one-half million casualties in the invasion of the whole island.
>
> None of the Marines and Army GIs out there knew that this weapon existed. Neither did I, incidentally. I knew that we were working on uranium. I never heard of it, and I was an analytical chemist. Whenever I thought of what I was doing in Oak Ridge, I knew that possibly great power could be released; but I was thinking in terms of ship-propulsion and things like that. I really didn't think about it very much at all, but it never occurred to me that they would make a bomb out of it.
>
> Anyway, the feeling of ending the war just made everybody so jubilant; they knew that the invasion would not be necessary. And all of the handwringing that's gone on since seems to ignore the point of what casualties American would have suffered if this had not happened. When you start a war, you can't always make the rules about how it's going to end. It's a shame, of course. A lot of people were killed—our people, too—and many hundreds of thousands more would have been killed.
>
> The only sense of shame I felt that night of celebration was that there never should have been any parties. No matter what happened, many thousands had died because of it, and that seemed to me the only fact in town that night.
>
> One bomb was dropped on the 6th, and the Japanese simply didn't know what had happened for a couple of days. Then, I think it was on the 9th,[2] the plutonium bomb was dropped on Nagasaki. By then, they listened to the radio and realized what had happened, and the emperor asked for surrender.
>
> I don't think of having dropped the bombs in terms of guilt. The only question I had was, "Were the Japanese given a chance to see the thing beforehand?" And I found out gradually over the years that, of course, that had been suggested. It had eventually been turned down by President Truman.
>
> The idea was of trying to stage a demonstration by inviting the Japanese to the bomb testing that same July.[3] I don't really know that it would have made

---

[2]Hiroshima was bombed August 6, 1945, U.S. time, and Nagasaki Aug. 9.

[3]The Los Alamos test was July 16, 1945.

much difference even if it could have been brought off and they could have gotten a Japanese observer to come. (This was in the middle of a very bitter war, and you can't get a message through.) You can't get somebody to take that sort of thing seriously. And if he had observed it and told what he saw, they wouldn't have believed it. Because it was just so absolutely beyond what anybody had ever seen before. For one man to go back to Japan and say, "Look, these people have this terrible bomb," in the mood Japan was in at that time—which was very much a mood of suicide—they would have said, "Come on!"

Five to eight thousand American people were being killed every day, and by shortening the war even one day, it saved many more killings. The Japanese didn't ask who was underneath when they bombed Pearl Harbor; and if you start a fight, you can't protest if it doesn't end the way it was intended to. The fire raids against Tokyo probably killed just as many.

In my interview with the Pomerances, I asked him how he felt when he heard that the bomb had been dropped, his feelings as a scientist having been involved in the production. Before I could finish my question, Ellie said, "Terrible!" Herb explained:

> Well, I guess it was several parts. One is that the petition had come around earlier for signing—should there be a demonstration?
>
> And we certainly were not against the bomb being tested or tried out. That it should be used on a city, as it was, is something else. I guess the ones who signed the petition felt that fair warning should be given. I think this must be close to the Alamogordo test. In fact, that was the only knowledge we had that the bomb was close. That was the only indication we had that something was coming up.
>
> We were at work the day the bomb was dropped. We heard the radio announcement that the bomb was dropped, and all we knew about it was what the wives of some of the fellows phoned in. And not every house had a phone in those days. They had phones on the streets for emergency calls and the section chiefs and higher had phones in the house.
>
> I don't think anyone felt theatrical like the Oppenheimers that we have known since. I think that, in a way, there was also a thankfulness that we weren't part of a $2 billion folly—that the thing had been successful. General Groves would have had his head cut off on the guillotine if it had failed.

Epilogue
The Coming of Age in Oak Ridge

To quote a line in my last letter to Margaret: "The honeymoon is over. It was nice while it lasted." Was Oak Ridge's coming of age spoiled by the emergence from slacks and muddy shoes to more sophisticated apparel, by transition from boardwalks to paved roads, to neon lights, motels, fast-food chains, and the usual trappings of our other more usual cities? By these standards, I suppose one could call Oak Ridge a "normal" city today.

Since 1948, our ties with Oak Ridge, our first home in East Tennessee, have been close. In fact, some of our best friends are Oak Ridgers. We, along with many others from nearby towns, have benefitted over the years from the outstanding cultural programs there. In all areas of the arts, Oak Ridge—with its comparatively small population of 30,000—was for a long time, and still is, way ahead of cities with a far greater number of inhabitants.

The character of Oak Ridge remains unique. From the rigid Army control of the reservation to the populace's do-it-yourself attitude, the city has been molded by its mix of people: the military, the unusually large group of intellectuals, combined with all the other sturdy citizens who simply "stuck it out." They, alone, have made it into what it is today. None of the cultural developments depended on the patronage or a power structure or on the philanthropy of wealthy contributors. There were no long-established elite families able to pride themselves on going back for generations. Instead, the social lines were of a completely different and unusual order. It was the enthusiasm of the young pioneers, brought together in one place at practically the same time, who participated in and supported high-quality, dynamic, and stimulating diversions. Even in the matter of education, the best was demanded, and the Oak Ridge schools rank as the top system in the region, if not the state.

197

Given the unexplained beginning and strange mission, what other city of comparable size can boast of achieving so much in its relatively short existence?

This "participating" city has had an extremely extensive musical life from the start. Now, under the umbrella of the Oak Ridge Music Association, the Orchestra, Community Chorus, Chamber Music Concerts—by both professional and local groups—and the like flourish. The Sunday Night Coffee Concerts are still a staple entertainment, with performers drawn from abundant local talent. Added to the musical advantages are such attractions as the long-standing Playhouse, the Ballet Company, and the Art Center (which, incidentally, sponsored Margaret Mead's visit to Oak Ridge in 1964).[1]

Oak Ridge was chosen by the national organization of the Recording for the Blind to be its regional headquarters; its operations are in the Margaret Despres Weinberg Center,[2] a lovely building, with the best equipment of its kind. Qualified readers, proficient in English and foreign languages, volunteer their services.

The Children's Museum, with its national reputation, has built up an unusual and varied collection, and is pointed out as a model for other communities. Its main emphasis is on the Appalachian region, with accompanying "artifacts," lecture programs, and archives.

Sports are popular and are an outgrowth of the Recreation and Welfare program sponsored by the Army throughout the war years. (Golf, interestingly, was not encouraged during the wartime period of secrecy because the game was considered to be too slow, thus allowing close fraternization and an opportunity to "talk," albeit inadvertently. Tennis was heartily encouraged; it is played with less "togetherness," and so was considered "safe" for security reasons.)

The Oak Ridgers are more than ordinarily aware and actively concerned

---

[1] By the time Mead finally made her first visit to Oak Ridge in May 1964 to give a lecture, she was able to draw on a large accumulation of material. She had established other contacts after—and, perhaps, before—we left Oak Ridge. (Although our correspondence ended then, we continued seeing Margaret and Gregory socially on our various trips to New York.)

The title of Mead's lecture was "Children in a Scientific Community," and it caused a stir. There were some people who felt she was justified in certain criticisms, and many others who felt hurt and resented several of her uncomplimentary remarks. They felt that some of her sweeping statements were superficial and based partly on "hasty" interviews during her two-day stay. (For *The Oak Ridger* accounts of her visit, see issues of May 15, 18, 19, 1968.)

As to how else anthropologist Margaret Mead used all the material on Oak Ridge, I can only quote from her letter to me on June 5, 1948: "It all does really get used, although sometimes in ways hard to document."

[2] This center is dedicated to Margaret Weinberg, whose untimely death was an irreplaceable loss to the Oak Ridge community.

about all phases of government, and are a strong political force in their county and in East Tennessee.

To be sure, Oak Ridge is no Utopia. Problems exist, as in all "normal" cities, and one may point to more than a few sobering realities. Perhaps these problems arose, in part, because the "overnight" city had to grow up too fast; maybe, too, because of its unique population with an inordinately high proportion of highly-educated people as opposed to those less-educated individuals who had come to work in Oak Ridge during the war and had stayed on.

Or could the problems have arisen because Oak Ridge is still a "company town" (although not in the ordinary sense)? No material goods are produced in its "factories." What comes out, mainly, is science and scientists. Added to the scientific production of the laboratories is the work of the Oak Ridge Associated Universities, which arranges for professors from universities throughout the South to spend time doing research in Oak Ridge and conducts training classes for qualified students in nuclear physics, chemistry and medicine. Then, too, Oak Ridge remains a town still dependent on federal supervision, now under the Department of Energy, which directs basic policies for the scientific area. Hundreds of jobs depend on whether or not Oak Ridge is to have a breeder reactor, for example.

Al Bissell has been the staunchest defender of nuclear power research and development. He calls Oak Ridge "a miracle city. If there were no Oak Ridge, we'd all be speaking German today."

He has nothing but praise for the people and community where he reared his family of five. "People used to say they were just going to be in Oak Ridge for a few years and then move on," he said. "Now they're finally calling Oak Ridge home. It's music to my ears."

As more positive national attention is focused on what the federal government accomplished at Oak Ridge, there are no apologies necessary from the twentieth-century frontiersmen like Al Bissell,[3] who came here in 1943. They occupied cinder-block government homes in a town that sprang up overnight. They turned government housing into a town that people now call home rather than a temporary assignment.

Oak Ridge remains unique. There is the inordinate, almost fierce, pride that the "doers" and citizenry have in what has been accomplished in their self-contained community. To these people who have put their roots down in Oak Ridge, this city was their "baby." Fundamentally devoted from its birth to science and research (and, perhaps through them, to the betterment of all society), this infant city has been reared by Oak Ridgers to a many-faceted and admirable youthhood.

---

[3]The sketch of Bissell and his remarks were taken from a column by David Lyons, the Knoxville *News-Sentinel's* Nashville correspondent. It appeared June 12, 1983, the year Mayor Bissell retired.